"A teacher shares the experience of his vibrant elementary school art class in a debut textbook with elements of memoir.

This engaging exploration of an Australian children's art course incorporates the work of Esling's young students as well as creative exercises that nascent artists will find valuable. Along the way, the author draws on years of experience teaching painting to elementary school students in Tasmania. It's mostly a teachers' manual, with Esling offering his thoughts on essential art materials and how to organize a classroom before launching into a series of art activities. Chapters include "Fun With Abstracts," "Painting Trees," and "Exploring Watercolours," with each exercise presented step by step; full-color photos by the author add to the instruction. The seasoned teacher also offers some hard-earned wisdom: "We miss the point of the journey if we cast judgment only upon the finished product," he writes at one point. "Just think for a moment of [the children's] personal qualities that have developed because of this creative exploration." The book is more than 300 pages long, but many, if not most, of them appealingly feature images of the students in action and charming photos of their finished products. Extras include a chapter that details a teacher's typical day at Esling's institution, Risdon Vale, from arrival at 8:15 a.m. to departure at 3 p.m., and helpful suggestions on where to display artwork within a school. Thanks to the author's winning way of conveying his love of teaching, this book works on multiple levels. Artists will enjoy the exercises, and teachers will easily be able to develop a semester's curriculum based on the thorough, almost diary like, classroom accounts. The book will even be enjoyed by those who have no interest in teaching or in how to be an artist; it's simply a compelling read that's a delightful combination of *Dead Poets Society and Making Art 101*.

Esling's appealing style makes for an exceptional instruction manual."

— Kirkus Reviews

Balboa Press books may be ordered through booksellers or by contacting:

Balboa Press
A Division of Hay House
1663 Liberty Drive
Bloomington, IN 47403
www.balboapress.com.au
AU TFN: 1 800 844 925 (Toll Free inside Australia)
AU Local: 0283 107 086 (+61 2 8310 7086 from outside Australia)

All photographs were taken by David Esling.
Original cover design by Marcus Gardner of Print Divsion, Hobart

ISBN: 978-1-9822-9501-1 (sc)
ISBN: 978-1-9822-9502-8 (e)

Print information available on the last page.

Balboa Press rev. date: 02/26/2023

CONTENTS

Foreword vii

Introduction..ix

Risdon Vale 1

My Early Days at Risdon Vale 3

Fun with Abstracts 11

In Praise of Composite Classes 46

A Typical Day at Risdon Vale 48

Mixing Powder Paints 1 49

Towards Our First Landscapes 51

Time for A Skill Trick or Two 67

Painting Trees 71

Painting Colours in Harmony and Contrast 84

Our First Landscapes 88

Mixing Powder Paints 3 107

Seeking Harmony and Contrast In Colours from The Rim of The Expanded Colour Wheel.....109

Books About Art and Artists.. 111

The Risdon Brook Dam 115

Adding Further Details... 122

Mixing Colours 4 131

From Painting Pictures with Words to The Expression of Thought and Feelings with Paint.....142

"Sometimes I Feel....." 148

From Pastels to Acrylic Paints...165

Paintings That Reflect Issues of Concern for Young People 174

The Concerns of Children from Risdon Vale 179

For Some, A Moment of Light Relief 192

What To Do Next 193

Richmond 194

Back At School 198

A Question of Ownership 212

Displays 213

Classroom Displays 219

The Risdon Vale Art Group 247

Beyond The Classroom Walls 267

Port Arthur 286

Back At School 290

Exploring Watercolours 295

A Christmas Cracker 307

Acknowledgements 319

FOR THE GOOD PEOPLE OF RISDON VALE
AND FOR ALL THOSE PEOPLE WHO LOVE TO WORK
ALONGSIDE CHILDREN

FOREWORD

GOING WITH THE FLOW

Dear reader, you recognise of course, that this is a work about teaching primary school children. The writer has been a pupil in independent schools in England and Tasmania. He endured periods when the teacher still had a dais, a platform, at the front of the room so that the teacher might look down in the effort to control and the pupils might look up and show attention. This book shows, in a detailed and illustrated way, the skilled work of someone who rejected the educational assumptions and the teaching practices which were standard in his childhood.

Let me introduce you to David Esling who began life in a family in England. David was sent to preparatory and independent secondary school where corporal punishment still held sway. The family migrated to Launceston, Tasmania where David was sent to the Grammar school which he found to be gentler and where his sporting prowess in cricket as a fast bowler gave him standing.

Next, he then went to study education at the University of Tasmania. During his school and university years he had the recurring thought that there were better ways to teach, and that there needed to be a way of paying much more attention to the activities of learning and that of the learner.

David has lived through a period when there were several attempts to formulate new approaches to teaching and the curriculum. In 1966 the English educator, Frank Whitehead, published 'The Disappearing Dais' a review of the teaching of English that stressed the activities of pupils in gaining a mastery of English. Whitehead claimed the role of the teacher was changing.

The physical relationship of teaching was changing; no longer was the teacher to look down on the class. Whitehead assumed that English was central, and the main purpose of the English teacher was not to instruct, but to provide a relaxed, friendly atmosphere in which the children could use and improve their language skills. The pupil was to be engaged which required the teacher to work alongside the learner. This, in turn, led the teacher to work alongside small groups.

David Esling built up sets of understanding and sensitivity to work alongside many learners. He became, at Risdon Vale primary school in a working-class area, a teacher who worked in workshop mode. The dais was gone but more importantly the dais mentality was gone. The matter of looking down no longer was an issue since he worked alongside the pupils seeking their observations and opinions.

This approach David (MrE) applied to working with art materials and focusing on the world alongside his pupils, the colour and the forms of the world. In the new dispensation he retains the right to point the pupils in a direction. On this occasion he began with the play and mix of colour which provides a rather abstract product yet one that all the pupils can follow at their own rate and still focus successfully on their individual ways.

This focus allowed pupils to have a wide range of options and explore the use of various materials and instruments. Colours can be explored while talking to each other and to MrE. The products of the pupils' efforts could be talked about and displayed and this in turn could give rise to further thought, reflection, and discussion. Pupils could have several attempts at explorations of colour their depictions might use.

The next step in the workshop sequence was the invitation to represent a tree. This was a choice of genius. There is a wide degree difference of shape and form of trees in the landscapes of Risdon Vale. Trees have varied, nuanced differences in shape and colouring, these were the centres of various discussions as representations were considered and tried, including how to depict various textures and the effects of light.

While they worked using different brushes in a variety of ways MrE played recordings of composers such as Bach and Vivaldi. He sought to engage the pupils with classical music. Some of his pupils were able to work with pupils in other classes in a style that followed that of MrE.

He used his camera to record and show the work in progress. Part of the work was displayed around the school and outside and led adults to take an interest in what was being produced in their school.

In this book MrE ends up beside the reader enjoying the events being described. His control, or rather his influence, is exercised in a more artful way than that he ever experienced as a pupil. Like the pupils he had to stay alert.

As they worked together, he and his pupils had conversations which enriched the language his pupils had at their command. David Esling is still remembered fondly by parents and pupils. The experiences he orchestrated were enlarging.

This work displays the achievements and joy of a teacher who abandoned the dais to display the learning possibilities of workshopping with the pupils. It also shows what happens when learners are encouraged to take an active role using powers of observation and reflection in their learning.

By now the reader will have realised I admire this work and MrE'S contribution to the profession of teaching.

Hugo McCann
Formerly Dean of Education, University of Tasmania, Hobart, Tasmania.

INTRODUCTION

In early 1952 our family moved from a country village to a working-class suburb "The Meadows" in Nottingham, England. We lived in Bathley St, similar in appearance to Coronation St of the television series. My father was the local vicar of the church 'St Faith's'. My playground was the street, and our meeting place was outside the local corner shop. My mother looked upon my newly found friends with disdain and discouraged me from playing with them.

"Those street kids are nothing but gutter snipes," she would say.

They were my only friends and there were no other kids to play with except for my two younger sisters. My mother spotted an advertisement in the 'Church Times' for a recently founded boarding school for boys called Knossington Grange Preparatory School. It was situated in a small country village about four miles away from Oakham in the county of Rutland. I was hurriedly enrolled and packed off to start the new school year in September 1952 a week before my eighth birthday.

The school was an old Manor House built of stone. It was very Gothic in appearance and had three floors and a basement. It reminded me of a castle with its huge dominant tower looming over a dark uninviting entrance hall. The upper walls were like the battlements of medieval castles. One could sense the archers hiding behind them as you approached the large wooden door that guarded the entrance. The surrounding grounds were expansive. There were open pastures, several spinneys and two lakes that were of course "Out of Bounds."

The headmaster had served as a merchant seaman crossing the Atlantic Ocean in numerous convoys to keep the supply chains open for the needy British people during World War Two. He was a strict disciplinarian and all our rooms had to remain in ship shape for countless inspections. In my first year, as a seven-year-old, my bedtime was 6-30 pm and my dormitory was on the first floor. It was named 'The Ark Royal after a few famous naval ships of the same name. The headmaster's study was two doors down the corridor, and we often had to line up there at bedtime to receive our weekly dose of the cane. The younger ones only received two strokes across the backside in their pajamas. When you were older you often received six of the best.

It was a cruel and unfriendly place. It was a struggle for survival and friends were hard to find. The bullies had a field day. The food was awful, but we were forced to eat it. The boys rarely asked for 'seconds. Eggs were boiled blue on Sundays and on Tuesdays, the scrambled eggs were much like a pale, yellow coloured blancmange. The school lessons were ghastly. We sat in three rows of six desks. Each Friday fortnight we had to suffer written tests to determine our place in class. Where we sat in class depended on the results of the previous Fortnightly Order.'

For most of the school day we would sit at our desks in silence watching and listening to the teacher standing in front of a blackboard or sitting at his desk on a raised platform. I often daydreamed of a class that was full of creative ideas for painting or making things with my hands.

My daydreaming often landed me in the queue outside the headmaster's study at bedtime. I tried in vain to remember the conjugation of Latin verbs, the endless dates of English Kings, the spelling of long words or endure the writing of compositions on matters that were of little concern to me. I was to stay at that school for six years and the only time I spent at home was at Christmas, Easter, and the long summer holidays.

My last two years at the preparatory school were more tolerable. I was near the top of the tree, and I was showing some skill at 'Games'. By 1956 I was playing rugby for the 'first fifteen' and was an opening bowler for the first cricket eleven. Without the success in sport, I doubt very much that I would have survived the ordeals of Knossington Grange. Several boys were unable to do so, and a few of them managed to escape under the cover of darkness into the wild countryside. Most of them were returned by morning but some of the escapees managed to find their way home, much to the amazement of their parents.

In September 1958, I was able to win a place at Oakham School. This was called a 'Public School' but was in fact a private school. Like many of the famous public schools it was founded in the 16th century. Oakham was founded in 1584 and remains open to this very day. The original schoolhouse is still in use today. In my time, it was used as a classroom but today it is more like a museum called 'The Shakespeare Centre.' I was in what was called 'the Middle School' which catered for boys from 14 to 16 years of age. The house in which I boarded was called 'Deanscroft' and that catered for boys aged from 14 to 19 years.

I started off in class 3B and after my fourth year I would have sat for my 'O levels'. Within a week of my arrival, I was appointed as a 'Fag' to one of the house prefects. In essence I was a servant to a sixth former and every time my duties were not up to scratch, I would receive a mark on the "Blacklist". When the long-suffering fag reached the tally of five black marks, the prefect would present a form for the housemaster to sign so that the prefect could beat me with a cane as I was bending over my own bed. So, once more I was standing on the bottom rung of the social ladder, just as it had been in my early days at Knossington. I also had to take care not to fall prey to the homosexual advances of some of the older boys. They were indeed tough times. That was the way of things. It was never questioned. There were no complaints.

The classroom life was like Knossington. In my home class, I sat at a desk in rows that indicated my place results in the recent series of tests. Learning was still a passive experience, and the retention of knowledge was the most desired outcome. Once again success with rugby and cricket proved to be my saviour. My housemaster often commented on my enthusiasm and bravery.

"It is character building," he used to say. "That's what we need, boys of good character, hey what!"

The housemaster sometimes made me feel that I was being prepared for future battlefields in foreign lands. Once a week in the afternoon, attendance at 'Cadets' was compulsory. We were dressed up in army uniforms, carried first world war rifles and were drilled along country lanes. We were being trained to be officers in an army for future wars. We were considered to be future leaders of men in combat. We were often reminded that we belonged to the elite. This had remained a salient feature of 'public school' life for centuries. In us lay the future of the Empire. Our participation in 'Cadets' was never questioned.

Before I sat my O Levels in the July of 1960 our family emigrated to Tasmania, Australia. It was a bold move for my parents with three teenaged children. I have often wondered why they made such a dramatic move. It may have been that they could no longer afford the fees to keep their three children at English boarding schools. It may have simply been a vocational choice of my father's. We set sail on the 'Orontes' from Tilbury on a wet July morning. Four weeks later we had arrived in Melbourne and on the following morning we set sail on 'The Princess of Tasmania for Devonport. It was still raining when we arrived at the Devonport railway station. It took a further two hours by the slowest train imaginable before we were met in Launceston by the appropriate dignitaries. It was still raining.

Within a week we had moved into our new house at St Leonard's and my father was soon inducted as parish priest of St Peter's. He also had to look after five other smaller parishes in nearby suburbs and country areas. It was demanding work and he had to purchase a second had car. Our house was limited with furnishings as we were yet to afford a fridge or a television set. My two sisters were enrolled at Broadland House, and I was sent to Launceston Grammar.

We were no longer boarders and that must have been a great relief for me, my sisters, and my parents. Our first task was to assimilate as quickly as possible into the Tasmanian way of life. That was not so easy for 'poms' with an uppity way of speaking. However, we soon picked up some useful Australian phrases such as 'Fair dinkum', 'Strewth,' and 'Cut the raw prawn'. As I spent most of my time at Grammar enjoying the view from the upper canopy of the learning tree, life was much kinder to me than at Oakham or Knossington. Senior classes in English and History were attended by less than twenty boys. There was much more time for healthy and lengthy discussion. We would often have fun taking a particular side of an argument such as 'State versus Church' in Tudor or Stuart England.

The heavy emphasis on English history in Australian schools puzzled me greatly at this time. It smelt like a throwback to colonial domination. The fact that we could speak our minds at Grammar restored a little of my faith in educational practice. However, I remember not having one art lesson at Grammar. It was not on my designated syllabus. The only time that I used my hands creatively was on the cricket field. Success in sport once again helped me enormously to be readily accepted by the Tasmanian community.

My sister Mary and I passed our Schools Board examinations in 1961. I was awarded a scholarship to continue my studies at Grammar and later won an Education Department Studentship that would cover the costs of a university education. I was at this time destined to become a schoolteacher. I still dreamed of working creatively in an open and friendly atmosphere, where learning could be fun and long lasting.

Throughout my school life there had been a preoccupation with testing. So much so, that teachers were simply teaching for better test results. This tyranny of testing put a strangle hold on many worthwhile learning experiences. Let us look at some of them. In England there was the 11+ that allowed you to an entrance to the junior section of a public school if your parents could afford it. If not, your results might have determined which stream you might have been placed in a state secondary modern school. That was followed by the Common Entrance Exams for thirteen-year-olds, to determine their suitability for entrance to the middle section of an English Public School. At the age of fifteen one sat for 'O' Levels followed by 'A' Levels a year or two later. If successful one might then win a place at a university. Then, the students would face four or five more years of annual examinations. Add to that, the run of the mill weekly or fortnightly tests to monitor your readiness to face the next round of examinations This preoccupation with testing would often streamline a curriculum down to its bare necessities and would leave little room for anything else.

It was similar in Australia. Primary schools had some form of annual standardised tests. I remember sitting for a Schools Board Certificate at the age of fifteen to soon be followed by two years of Matriculation exams. If one was lucky, one might have found a place at a university and suffered the stresses of examinations for four more years. Of course, I accepted that testing played and still plays a useful role in the educative process, but really, do we need so much of it? There are other means by which children, teachers and schools can be evaluated.

Have we made much progress over the last few decades? I don't think so. Look at the current situation in Australian Primary Schools today for example. We have a national system of standardised testing to check the progress of children, teachers, and schools. Children are tested every two years to hopefully illustrate their progress with literacy and numeracy. Schools are rewarded for showing improved results. The natural consequence being, that teachers are spending an increasing amount of time preparing children for these tests and once again we see that the curriculum is being stripped to its bare bones. I asked a current primary school teacher recently if she had recently tried some creative artwork.

Her reply was, "I think I did some a month or two ago. Maybe, sometimes on a Friday afternoon as a kind of treat for the children. There are now more important matters that require our attention."

I am sure that she was referring to literacy and numeracy. "We have not progressed very far, have we?"

When I started teaching in 1967, we often did some art on Friday afternoons. They were simple 'one off' sessions where the work would have been completed within the one session. We tried to avoid messy activities though, as that would have prevented a quick getaway at three o'clock. In those days we should have done much better, as we were then not suppressed under the stresses and strains of 'NAPLAN'.

Some of the better creative teachers today are gradually leaving the classroom. There is no longer sufficient time or room for them. It would have been unlikely for some to become specialist art or drama teachers in other schools. I know of some teachers who have become so disillusioned that they are considering leaving the profession altogether. This madness has got to stop. I believe every primary school teacher should be using 'Art' in their classroom on a regular basis. There should be no need for a 'specialist art teacher' in the primary school. Every teacher should be a teacher in 'ART' and he doesn't need to be an artist to achieve that. Art permeates through so much of a worthwhile curriculum and in particular the world of mathematics.

I can only remember two teachers during my schooldays who influenced me in an artistic way. Other than that, I have never had an art lesson in my life. The significance of 'Art in Education' was drawn to my attention in 1966 during my studies in education by a Mr. Ken Thomas. It was the only time at University I was to be involved in any practical learning by using my hands. Ken twice visited me during my early days as a teacher and he was most encouraging. In 1972, I stayed at his home in Sheffield, England after his return to the mother country. Ken showed me around several progressive schools in Yorkshire and his influences largely forged my future directions and practice in education.

I must freely admit that when I began teaching in 1967, I began by being the teacher I did not want to be. It was then the only way I knew.

My first class cared for forty - two students so my options were limited. I stood in front of the class and was for a time 'a formal teacher'.

"Give them tests to do. It is a good way to keep them quiet and under control," the headmaster advised me on my first day.

I was expected to do just that. Gradually over a couple of years, I found ways to break away from the constraints of formalised teaching. I decided then and there, that if I wanted to be a teacher, I would have to work towards a creative approach to teaching and learning that would not suffer under the tyranny of testing. I began by showing and developing an interest in creative writing. Instead of imposing a subject for composition, I would seek ways that would stimulate the children to write. It might have been a poem or story concerning aspects of children growing up. It might have been the tasting of a lemon or a similar assault on the senses. It sometimes might have been a reflection of one of their own experiences. The essential feature was that the children were writing about what mattered to them and for someone who mattered to them. Hopefully, that someone would have been the teacher from time to time. It was not long before children were bringing to school their own short pieces of writing that were written in their own homes under their own initiative. Some of them may have been in the form of a poem.

My Mother

She left one sorrowful day.
Three children she left behind her.
She wished that she could stay
but there was no other way.

Selina C 11

By 1971 I had built up a reputation as an enthusiast for children writing creatively. I was invited to be a guest speaker at the annual Principals' Conference at Port Sorell. At the same time, I was asked to represent Tasmania by writing a chapter for a book on creative writing in Australia. The book had the rather pompous title "My Machine Makes Rainbows. Each chapter was written by a teacher from each of the Australian States. As the reputation grew, I was asked to speak at the University and the Advanced College for teachers in training. For a few years, I led teachers in three-day writing workshops at teachers' centres around the state in Hobart, Launceston, and Burnie.

From 1973-5 I taught at Lenah Valley Primary School. It was a lovely place to live and teach. My classroom was the old infant section. It was a double sized classroom. My imagination ran wild with so much available space for a class of about thirty grade six children. The principal David Hunt was fully supportive and encouraged me to explore ideas for a more open approach to teaching and learning. I still retained my interest in creative writing, but I was wary of being pigeon - holed as a specialist. I looked forward to extending my creative approaches by including the world of Art and Mathematics. I had to find my own way. A lot was learned by trial and error. By the time I left Taroona Primary School in 1992, I was almost there. I had planned and implemented several artistic explorations that included Painting Landscapes, Portraiture and working with Clay. I had also planned and implemented many creative explorations in the field of Mathematics that included Linear, Square and Cubic Measurement.

I had purchased a decent camera and photographed the story of many an exploration. Thus, over time, I built up an extensive visual and written record of many creative and explorative investigations. Working at the middle - class Taroona was a stimulating and demanding experience for me. The children lived in an environment that was advantageous for them. Most of them were very intelligent and a teacher had to work hard to satisfy their intellectual needs and demands. In 1993 by my request, I took up a teaching post at Risdon Vale Primary School. The differences between the two schools could not have been greater. I had to find a way to engage the children, to make them feel that they wanted to come to school. At first, they were hostile within themselves and towards each other. My early days with them were very difficult. I chose some of my artistic explorations to help us through this difficult time. The artistic explorations were further developed and refined during my seven years at Risdon Vale. Through artistic explorations I found a way to reach the children. Working with 'Abstracts' was my first big success. The children felt the joy of success, and everything was able to flow on from there. They wanted to come to school again. Their self-esteem began to rise and consequently their behaviour improved.

Sometimes, working creatively with the children of Risdon Vale was quite stressful. During a creative exploration one had to be constantly evaluating, monitoring the progress of the creative idea, the manner of the children working together, the suitability of the noise level, the appropriate verbal responses given to and by the children.

I was constantly thinking on my feet. I was flying by the seat of my pants. I found it often exhilarating, working on the knife's edge so to speak. However, the risk taking could also be very tiring. Sometimes, I would raise my voice and shout to keep the excessive noise under control when the tinkle of a bell might have been the better option. I had no wish to upset neighbouring teachers who preferred the peace and quiet. I found the playing of recorded light classical music was a very useful tool to help the control of excessive noise. I would play some Bach or Vivaldi and if I could not hear the music at any given time, I would let them know by the tinkle of a bell. The children also felt relaxed hearing the music and would often try to turn up the volume. Fancy that, the melodies of Bach and Vivaldi being acceptable in the valley of Heavy Metal, Punk and Rap.

During and at the end of each explorative journey we would stop and turn to admire the view. As we walked around our classroom gallery, we reminded ourselves that the journeys themselves were of greater significance that the joys of reaching a particular destination. During our explorative journeys we had all learned so much. In the galleries we just glowed with pride.

This book "A FLOWING THROUGH" tells the story of some of my artistic explorations with the children of Risdon Vale. By the time I left Risdon Vale in 2000, I had re-modelled my creative approaches down to a fine art. Working with composite classes enabled me to work on a two-year programmer that covered artistic explorations in the fields of Painting, Drawing, Paper Art, Clay, Portraiture and Still Life. Each strand of exploration began with a simple starting point and often flowed through to destinations that far outreached earlier expectations. It was quite common for the children themselves to initiate the directions that we were to follow. We were all teachers and learners. We were all explorers each in need of support from each other. Each year the teacher tried to introduce a new field of exploration to ensure a continuation of fresh ideas. The progress of each exploration was recorded with photographs and written notes, thus providing the foundations of this book. By the time I left Risdon Vale in 2000. I finally had become the teacher that I wanted to be so long, long ago. There was no further need for daydreams.

David Esling Hobart, Tasmania,   February 2021.

RISDON VALE

The community began in the late 1950's as a housing commission settlement; a brain wave of the Tasmanian Government, that offered affordable housing for the lower socio-economic strata of our society. It was surrounded by hills on three sides and the River Derwent bordered the western side. A sheltered recluse one might say, well hidden from the middle-class neighbouring suburb of Lindisfarne. Since those early days, six more settlements of a similar nature have popped up on the eastern shore. Nearby, lay the site of the first European settlement in 1803. The swampy land was found to be unsuitable for the early Europeans and some months later it moved to nearby Hobart Town. In the 1950's Risdon Vale swampy rivulet was reclaimed and soon the site boasted a shopping centre and buildings essential for community services. Newly built weather board houses sprang up like spring flowers alongside roads that were named after well-known plants. E.g.: Gardenia, Heather, Fuchsia, Banksia etc.:

A primary school was built nearby and opened in 1960.The community spread at an alarming rate and by 1962 the school cared for over 1000 children. More blocks of classrooms were built to house the inevitable increase of children and by 1969 the school population had peaked at over 1300 children. The school must have been so difficult to manage at that time. With government support, the community services also grew to support the growing needs of so many young families. Most of the families would have paid a nominal rent to the "government for the pleasure of living in Risdon Vale. At the hub of all this was the Neighbourhood Centre surrounded by the local shopping centre, the hairdressers, fuel stations, fast food shops and a betting shop. Close by was the football and cricket oval and a community hall. On the edge of Risdon Vale stood the local pub and within sight of this, the government built the State Penitentiary.

With the passing of time the community matured and there were many families of three generations living in the area. As community members aged, the number of children declined. By the time I arrived in 1993, the school population had fallen to about 300 children. The decline was so great that classroom blocks had been removed only to reappear in a similar yet younger communities a few km further north. The Risdon Vale school now had a new giant concrete playground. A remaining weatherboard classroom block that housed my classroom had an empty room next door. There was an open archway to allow freedom of movement from one room to another.

I loved the extra space, and the adjoining room soon became an extension of my classroom. The school population continued to fall and by 2020 it was about 165 and rumours of possible closure began to spread like unwanted weeds. Despite the difficulties they faced, the Risdon Vale Community had done much to help themselves. They were not a community of 'bludgers', and they were very proud of their modest achievements. Many had taken advantage of the government's buy back scheme. Instead of rent, their monthly payments gradually paid off the purchase of their own houses. By 2020 more than half of the community had bought their own homes. However, COVID 19 had reared its ugly head and many of the casually employed found work and income difficult to maintain. Services provided by the Neighbourhood centre had to be seriously modified. No longer was it possible to continue with meetings of the 'Art Group' or any other such groups. Instead, the centre had to spend most of its time organizing the delivery of food parcels to those in need. By the end of 2020, the future looked a little brighter. New houses were being built on recently subdivided land. Perhaps, a new generation would hopefully come to the rescue.

MY EARLY DAYS AT RISDON VALE

After a week or two at Risdon Vale, I soon had an idea of the job in front of me. Some of the children, like their parents before them, clearly gave the impression that they did not want to be at school. Their body language clearly amplified this negative attitude. Their rather uncouth speech showed little care for themselves or each other. They were angry within themselves and with each other. Their self-esteem was seriously low. Their social skills were combative rather than co-operative. Some had already succumbed to the notion that they were failures. Some looked for ways to disrupt our learning activities and then encouraged the cheering approval of their peers. I felt so sorry for the children who still wished to learn and for those who still hoped that school might lead them towards a more fulfilling life. No wonder the school was primarily involved in behaviour management. I first looked to attract the interest of some reluctant learners and troublemakers. I called the class into the reading corner for a little chat.

I began by telling them a little about the school I attended when I was their age. I told them that I was sent to a boarding school at the age of seven and remained there until I turned fifteen. I spoke of harsh discipline, strict teachers and boring lessons, awful food, and early bedtimes.

I told of fortnightly tests and how we sat at single desks in rows that reminded you of your place in the class. We all knew our place in the order of things. I hated school, it was a lonely place, a place where bullies thrived. I longed for a school that allowed children to be active and practical. I wanted to use my hands. I wanted a school where you could openly discuss your shared learning experiences. I dreamed of a school where learning was fun.

"You know what? I think the school that I lived in over forty years ago was far worse than the school that you seem to dislike today. It doesn't have to be that way. We can change things around. You and I can make a difference. We all can, together," pleaded their teacher.

"But how?"

"I think we could try a lot of creative work that might help us to feel better within ourselves and with each other. I can think of several activities that would ensure success over failure, excitement over boredom and hope over despair. I think I can make you want to come to school again. However, I will need help from all of you. Surely, it is worth a try. Don't you think?"

"Do you mean we will do more Art, MrE?"

"Yes! to some extent we can do more art; but we can also be creative by making things with our hands e.g.: making balloon powered cars out of shoe boxes or be involved with creative explorations of a mathematical nature. When did you last have some fun with artistic explorations?" the teacher asked.

"Last year we did some art on some Friday afternoons if we had finished our other work."

"I don't remember doing much art since I was in Grade 2, and we never did any exploring."

"Learning can be fun, I promise you. Shall we give it a go then? I will need your support to make it work. You will have to be supportive of each other and freely offer praise and encouragement to everyone."

"Yes! Yes! Yes!" Their enthusiastic response echoed from wall to wall.

"Good we shall start tomorrow afternoon," added the teacher. "We shall begin with the painting of 'ABSTRACTS' by running water through powder paints."

And so began our series of artistic explorations at Risdon Vale primary school.

The Mysterious "MrE"

Long ago, back in 1971 in my fourth year of teaching, I was approached by a group of children as we walked out for lunch.

"Why can't we call you David? You call us by our first names, so why can't we.?"

I was somewhat taken aback. For a moment I did not know what to say.

"That's one of the loveliest compliments I have so far received in my career. Let me think on it for a while."

I discussed the request with my colleagues over lunch.

"The trouble with you David, is that you are too familiar with the children. They will be in control of you before too long and then there will be absolute chaos. Where is the respect that they should have for teachers?"

"I thought respect was something we had to earn rather than demand," I replied.

"Absolute poppy cock."

"I thought that it was out of respect for me as a teacher that I was asked if they could use my first name."

"Absolute rubbish, David. Think about the rest of us. How do you think we would feel, if you allowed them to call you David?"

I returned to class and thanked the children for their kind request.

"I thought it was a great honour to be asked. Thank you, but I must decline your request. However, let's consider a compromise. How about calling me MrE?"

I then wrote 'MYSTERY' on the blackboard. We all had a good laugh. The nickname stuck and since then I have been called 'MrE' for the rest of my career. Some of my friends still call me by that name and I have been retired for twenty years.

MAINLY PAINTING

Painting provides us with a means of expressing what we see. The images we paint might show others how we think and feel about what we see.

Children from an early age love playing with splashes of colour, shape and pattern. However, their naturally creative play needs some supportive scaffolding as they approach middle primary school. With that support, a continued purposeful growth in their appreciation and participation in the world of 'art' can be assured.

"What materials do we need for the general classroom?"

"What simple skills can be acquired that are both useful and fun for learning?"

Children are taught some progressive skills as they play the sports they love. There are skills in abundance required as some children learn to play a musical instrument. So, it should naturally follow that some artistic skills are learned as children experience a variety of creative explorations. Ideally, we don't need specialist art teachers in schools as every Primary School teacher should be building up a simple set of artistic skills required to inspire further explorations. I hope that this book will provide teachers with some of these skills and the stories of the artistic explorations will I trust, inspire many teachers to follow in our footsteps.

ESSENTIAL ART MATERIALS FOR THE GENERAL CLASSROOM

BRUSHES

Large house paint brushes 50mm and 25mm for washes and large backgrounds
Round Bristle brushes........sizes 2,4,6,8,19,12 for backgrounds, dabbing, and rolling.
Flat Bristle brushes.... Sizes 4,6,8,10
Small Bristle and soft haired brushes sizes 3,5,8,10 for adding detail.

All these brushes can be used with Powder Paints, Acrylic and watercolours. Late in the year some children would follow their teacher and bring their own good quality brushes to school.

A closer look at some soft haired brushes from MrE's collection.

Here we see a child using a teaspoon to transfer small amounts of powder paint from a container to a mixing tray.

PAINTS

Tins of Powder Paint (Red, Yellow, Blue, Black, and White)
2 Litre Plastic Containers of Acrylic Paint
(Primary and Secondary Colours with Black and White)

PAPER

LITHO (shiny on one side) Size A3 and A4 for drawing and paint mix testing

CARTRIDGE A3 and A4 for painting

CARDBOARD A3 White and possibly Black

PENCILS

Soft 2B, 4B, 6B, Medium HB, Hard 2H.

THINGS

Clean water containers, Plastic Plates for paint mixing, Sponges, wipes, rags, and mops for cleaning.
Plastic spoons for transporting paint to mixing trays.

THE GEOGRAPHY OF OUR CLASSROOM

Our classroom was arranged to facilitate group learning and healthy discussion about the matters at hand. The Reading Corner apart from being our centre for reading was also our meeting place for honest discussions concerning the progress of our classroom life. The classroom belonged to us all; our progress was for the benefit of us all and the rewards must be shared by us all. We had a collective ownership. We all had a part to play. The teacher was, for the most part, acting as the leader.

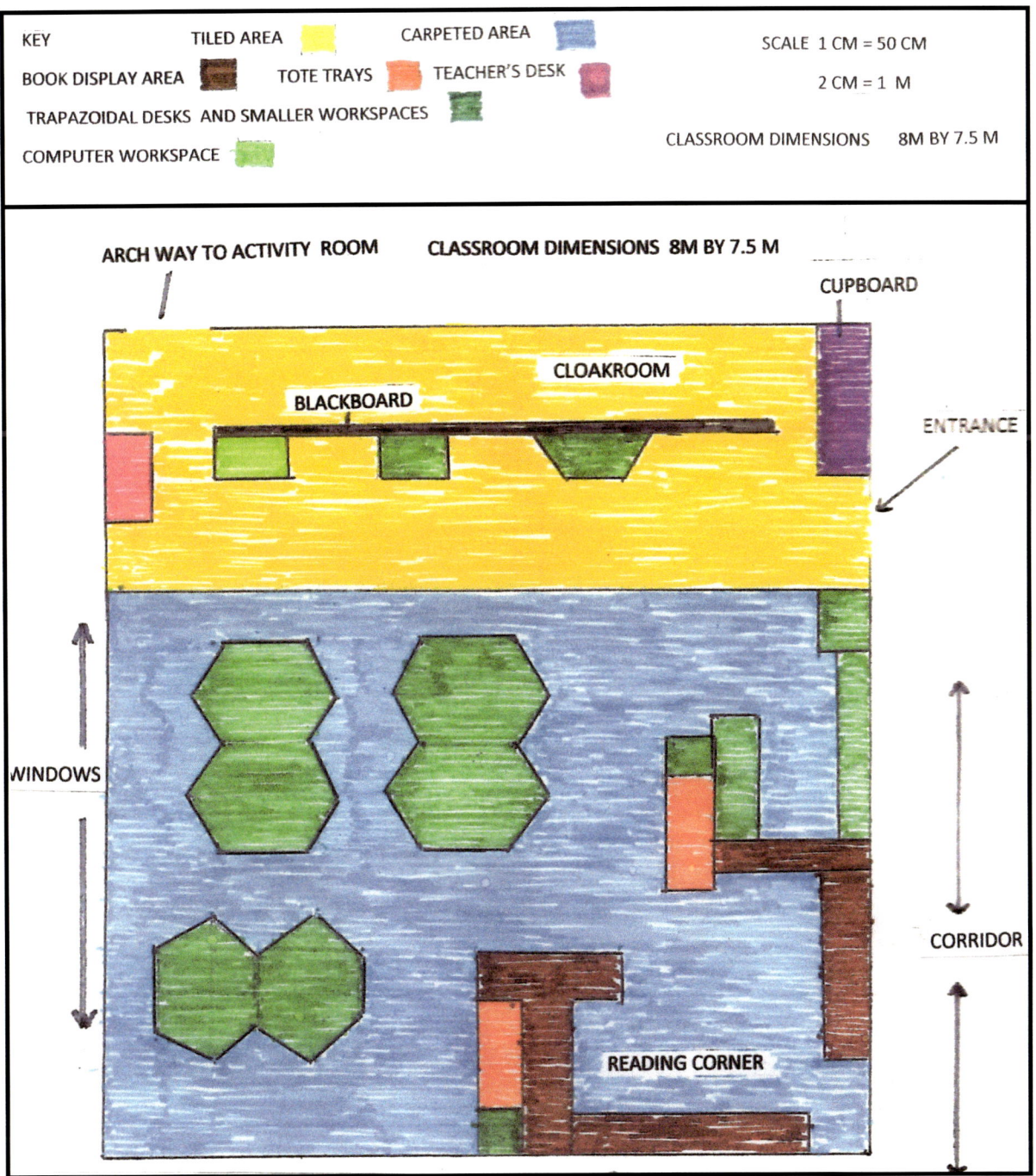

NOTES

The book display area in the reading corner was made up of magazine shelves for the larger reference or storybooks and the two areas against the wall were made up of old unwanted desks covered with coloured hessian. The space underneath stored learning materials and some of their large artistic folders.

There was only one computer housed in the classroom. Preference was given to children who wished to use 'Word'

The teacher's desk proved to be a most useful workspace for activities in the latter half of each day, e.g.: Art activity or for solving practical challenges such as making a bridge out of a restricted amount of paper and cardboard.

The trapezoidal tables provided ample space for collaborative learning groups while the remaining desk space was available for children wished to work alone or in pairs.

The children did not have their own desks. Instead, they housed their personal tools of learning in a large tray. A chest of trays was called a Tote tray.

FUN WITH ABSTRACTS

1 Running Water Through Powder Paint

For our first explorative journey into the world of ABSTRACTS, I chose the idea of running water through powder paint. This activity was quite easy to do and only needed close supervision in the early stages. It was an ideal choice for some of the reluctant learners as the children needed a 'Wow!' factor to win their interest and ensure a taste of success.

MATERIALS NEEDED

Six to eight easels, sponges and rags, masking tape, large housepaint brushes, medium to large bristle brushes, assorted colours of powder paints, paint containers, small buckets of water, grey or black marker pens, charcoal sticks, sheets of A3 cartridge paper or thin white cardboard, mops and wipes.

STAGE 1

I began by working with a group of about six boys and girls and deliberately included some with a livelier disposition than most. Limited materials necessitated a small group approach, but I also wished to generate as much discussion as possible as we travelled through the early stages. Trying to do this with the whole class at once would only have invited a disaster. Our principal, Brendon, was invited to care for the class while the teacher worked with a small group next door in the activity room. The room was tiled and was ideal for a messy activity. Six easels were set up ready for use.

It was vital to have all the materials close at hand before the teacher began his demonstration. The essence of success was 'SPEED.' The top of a sheet of A3 cartridge paper was lightly affixed to the top of the easel with masking tape. The chosen few were standing close by eagerly watching the teacher's every move. A large house paint brush laden with water, was brushed across the paper in sweeping left to right movements.

Immediately, a large bristle brush dipped in powder paint was applied to the wet paper with some sense of colour choice and balance. The teacher talked through the techniques as he was demonstrating the early stages of his painting.

"Can you see the paint running down the paper?"

"Yes, I can. It's running down to the floor."

"That's ok, we shall mop that up after I have finished."

A large house paint brush laden with water was then pressed against the top of the paper and the water trickled down the paper and through the powder painted areas.

"Can you see the runs of watery paint now? They look like tide marks. That is the effect we are looking for. Now watch this?" their teacher asked of them.

The paper was carefully removed from the easel and stuck back at an angle of about 45 degrees. More paint and water were then applied to the paper.

"Wow! That looks great. The funny lines are running in all directions," said Mitchell.

The paper was very carefully removed from the easel and left to dry in a safe place. The messy floor was wiped clean.

"Just remember, wet paper is easily torn," MrE concluded.

The children were itching to try it themselves. The easels, paper, brushes, and paint were already set up for them.

"Now have a try yourselves. There is a spot for each of you. I'll come back in a minute or two to see how you are going," said MrE.

The teacher revisited the classroom. All was going well. The main body of the class knew that it would be their turn soon. The teacher returned to the activity room to find that the group of six had nearly completed the first stage. This stage had to be completed within five or six minutes to ensure an excellent flow of water runs.

"Damien, that's looking great. The water from that brush is causing a lot of tidemarks. Try not to use too much paint as the tide marks might all be covered up. If you want, you can move the paper around again. Remember, it is the effect of running water through paint that makes the picture so interesting," added MrE..

After a quick clean-up it was time for some others to have a turn. However, their teacher had withheld a little surprise for the first group of six.

"Before you return to the classroom, I wonder if any of you might like to act as tutors for another group of six children?" All of them willingly agreed if it was one child for each tutor

"Can we choose the person to work with?"

"That's fine, but just remember the ideas and techniques that I was encouraging you to follow," replied MrE.

They seemed very happy and confident with the arrangement and the teacher felt free to spend more time with the fifteen children remaining in the classroom. He still however, kept a close eye upon the tutors and learners. The tutors were excellent. They just knew what to say and how to say it. The tutors were justly proud of themselves, and the learners were well satisfied with their first forays into fun with abstracts. The teacher felt an inner glow of warm satisfaction.

Sarah is guiding Tony to release water from a housepaint brush

An excellent array of tidemarks.

Within a few minutes half the class had been able to complete their first set of water runs through powder paint. After the cleanup, there was little time left in our school day. The teacher assured the rest of the class would have their turn the following afternoon. This was our beginning of a pattern of teaching and learning that was to become prevalent in our classroom life.

After their half-finished paintings had dried, the children wrote their names on the bottom right corner of the sheet of A3 paper or cardboard. By the end of the following afternoon, the process was repeated for the children still awaiting their turn. The teacher again demonstrated the opening approach to a group of six volunteers knowing that they too would be asked to act as tutors. By the end of the second afternoon everyone had completed the first stage of at least one powder paint abstract. However, we were not yet finished.

The activity room was the perfect location as the floor was tiled. The inevitable mess was easily mopped up.

STAGE 2

A few days later, MrE used his demonstration piece from stage 1 to help him explain the second stage of Powder Paint Abstracts. To save time he found a way to demonstrate to the whole class at once. He placed himself at a table so that a dozen children could sit around the table. The remainder were able to stand behind those who were seated. They all waited with eager anticipation.

The teacher had nearby a selection of black and grey marker pens and a few charcoal sticks of variable size. He carefully showed them how to accentuate some of the tide mark lines on the painting. Some with thick bold lines and some with thin, some with grey and some with black.

Year six Sarah tutors a year five girl with the charcoaling of her painting.

When they were free to do so, the children finished their paintings by adding accentuated lines. Their works appeared to be most effective. They were delighted with their paintings and were thrilled to see them trimmed, mounted, and displayed.

The classroom walls above the eyeline were filled with children's works of art. Some of their work on display overflowed to cover the walls of the activity room. It was interesting to note that the echoing sounds that bounced off the classroom walls had diminished. The acoustics were much improved, and we were only in the middle of the fourth week of the school year.

The use of charcoal sticks proved to be a popular choice. It took a long time for Jessica to charcoal the tidemarks over her intricate design. Her patience and perseverance were well rewarded with the creation of an excellent work.

The children who were in their second year with us, year six that is, mounted their own work for display. It was not long before the older children showed the newcomers how to mount their own work. The roles of child tutors seemed to be forever expanding.

As soon as their works were double mounted, they were displayed on the classroom walls, in the corridor and the activity room.

A group of children expressed a wish to show their paintings to children in other classes. A visit was soon arranged and a spokesperson or two explained their approaches from the early beginnings until the successful outcomes.

Nicole was appointed spokesperson and Haylee helped her tell the story of their paintings
"Did you enjoy showing your paintings to other children in our school?" asked MrE.
"Yes, it felted real good MrE. Can we do that again?" asked Charles.
"I'm sure we will. I felt really good about it as well," replied his teacher.

The teacher could feel their growth in confidence. Their self-esteem was on the rise, and they were beginning to feel that they mattered after all. They were all surprised and overjoyed with the quality of their paintings.

"Oh! what a feeling." The proud explorers were on their way. They eagerly awaited their next exploration.

I used this idea of running water through powder paint every second year whilst I was at Risdon Vale from 1993-2000. In the alternating years I used the idea of combing instruments through acrylic paints to create an equally stunning set of abstract paintings. The beauty of 'Abstracts' is that they rarely look 'wrong'. They are easy to do, and success is virtually guaranteed. Here follows a gallery of paintings selected from the three times that we embarked on this explorative journey, "Running water through powder paint."

GALLERY WALK

Sharyn 10

Some of the children could see things in their abstract paintings and then they tried to emphasise them with a dark line. Charles insisted that there was a face in his painting. He pointed out to me the eyes, nose, mouth, and neck. It took more than a second look to find them.

Blair gave her painting the feel of a landscape. With a little imagination one could identify the distant clouds, the background hills, and the lush green foreground with a tree or two.

Charles 11

Blair 10

Jamie 10

Jessica 11

Emma 10

Chloe 10

Malinda 10

Sarah 10

Julian 10

Some cynics might suggest that the finished products looked a little like wallpaper.

"Ah! but wonderful wallpaper."

We miss the point of the journey if we cast judgement only upon the finished product. Just think for a moment of their personal qualities that have developed because of this creative exploration. The explorers have learned to give and receive support from one another. Those who acted as tutors developed their communicative skill. They had picked up the language of their teacher. They had become more articulate. Their shared discussions reflected a growing respect for one another. They felt valued and that they mattered after all. Most of all their self-esteem was given a huge boost. Their paintings looked just great. I remember Malinda when she was in year five and as she was looking at her painting on the wall said,

"That's me up there. I did that MrE."

So, school could be a fun place once again. We still had most of the year in front of us. There was still so much to do before we could harvest the joys of further achievements.

MAP OF THE ACTIVITY ROOM

The activity room was formerly a general classroom when the school catered for over a thousand children. Nowadays it was completely tiled and was a shared working space by its two neighbouring classrooms. It was ideally suited for small groups of children engaged in practical explorations. The room housed three large tables and two large activity trolleys that held the necessary tools, materials, and equipment. There was a shelf underneath each table that held coloured cover paper, and large sheets of cartridge paper. The tables were covered with coloured plastic 'contact' so that it could be easily wiped clean.

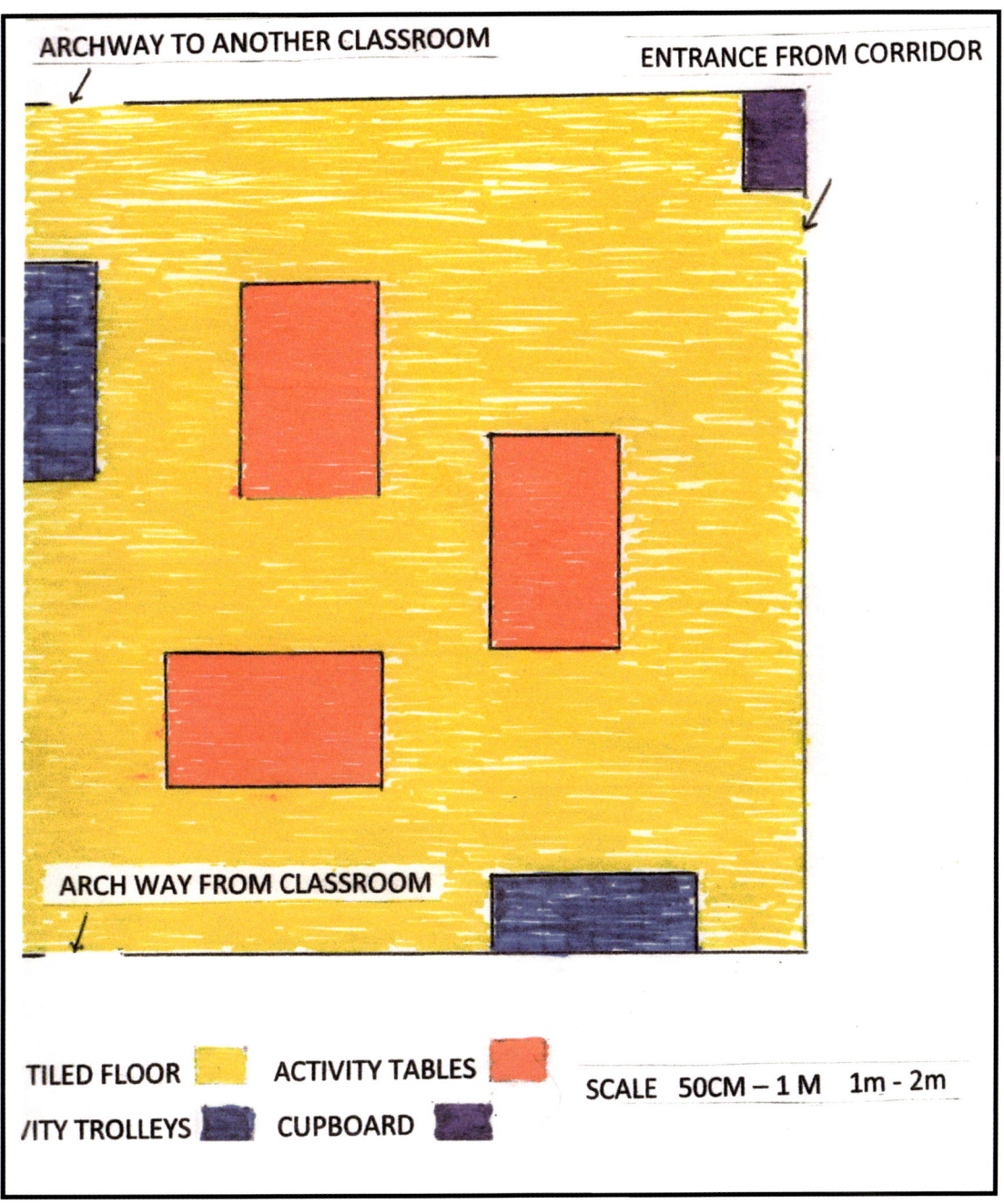

FUN WITH ABSTRACTS

2 Acrylic Paintings

Each successive year I would alternate "Abstracts with Powder Paints" and "Abstracts with Acrylic Paints." The beauty of exploring "Abstracts" was that there was no clear division between what might appear to be right or wrong. Therefore, the children were more positive and confident in their approaches to this manner of painting. They did not feel so inadequate by saying, "This doesn't look right," and let slide their interest and desire to continue with the painting. Instead, they embraced the challenge and trusted their teacher to lead them further into the world of Abstracts. This exploration was also a great one to try early in the school year. The taste of success was almost guaranteed. It was success for the children that was so much in need. The savouring of success would help to lift their self-esteem and make them feel that their school was a great place to be.

We began by practicing some simple tasks using thick, creamy acrylic paints that held both texture and vivid colours. We called these tasks "Skill Tricks", a term I used to conjure up a sense of magic. Some of these exercises materialised as mounted paintings, so pleasing were they to the mind and eye.

MATERIALS NEEDED

PAINTS

Junior Non-Toxic Acrylics in 2 litre containers
Red, Green, Blue, Yellow, Brown, Black and White.

BRUSHES

Large and medium House Paint Brushes Bristle Brushes Round and Flat
Sizes - Large, Medium, and Small

PAPER

Cartridge Paper A3 size or preferably Sheets of White Cardboard A3 size.
Cut out cardboard Combs with teeth of variable size and shape.

THINGS

Icy pole sticks, Flat headed Nails, or any other implements useful for dragging, pulling, or pushing through paint.
Plastic tea and tablespoons

SKILL TRICKS

1 DRAGGING CARDBOARD COMBS THROUGH PAINT

A black background was painted over a white sheet of cardboard. A large house paint brush was used to brush the paint in sweeping left to right movements across the sheet of cardboard to maintain an even line and grain.

"That's the idea Stefan, try a full sweep right across the sheet and don't stop until you have passed the right edge, suggested MrE.

A tablespoon was then used to drop dollops of paint on two or three locations over the background while it was still wet. A teaspoon was then used to drop smaller dollops of contrasting paint over the top of a previously dropped dollop. A ready-made cardboard comb was then dragged or pushed through the paint to create a pleasing shape or pattern.

2 TEASING OUT PATTERNS WITH ICY POLE STICKS ETC

For this exercise or skill trick, it was not necessary to paint a background. Dollops of paint were again dripped and blobbed on to the white cardboard. However, instead of using a carboard comb, other utensils were used to tease out shapes and patterns. The teacher witnessed the use of Icy pole sticks, Flat headed nails, plastic knives, and forks.

"That's it, tease out the shapes from near the centre of the dollop of paint and tease it outwards over the sheet of cardboard. I have noticed that some of you have created some shapes that look a little like a starfish," added MrE.

Some children then lightly spun or twirled a bristle brush in the centre of a dollop of paint for a special effect. They were taking risks, they were experimenting. They were learning from their interactive play. Some children continued to drop more dollops of paint. They were having fun exploring so many of the possibilities before them. Some were bold and brave explorers while some others just stood back for a while and observed what was happening around them, hoping to pick up a good idea. There was an excitable flow of conversation as they shared their little discoveries. The teacher liked what he heard and saw before his eye. He picked up his camera and took a photo or two. We were all witnesses to a show of creative play and exploration.

"What else did Mr E see through the eye of his camera?"

3 TWIRLING LARGE ROUND BRISTLE BRUSHES

A large bristle brush coated with one or two acrylic colours was pushed, turned, and twirled as it slid across the paper or cardboard. It helped if the brush was lightly held in the hand. Sometimes the turns and twirls were reversed enabling a brush to move in another direction.

4 A COMBINATION OF SKILL TRICKS

A few children practiced a combination of 'Skill Tricks' on to one sheet of paper or cardboard. They were then confident enough to apply them to carefully chosen backgrounds.

POPULAR BACKGROUNDS

In this example, large house paint brushes were used so that more than one colour softly merged into another.

Here we see a double background. After a dark background had dried; a pink one was superimposed over it. While still wet, the pink second background was scratched with a cardboard comb to create some attractive patterns.

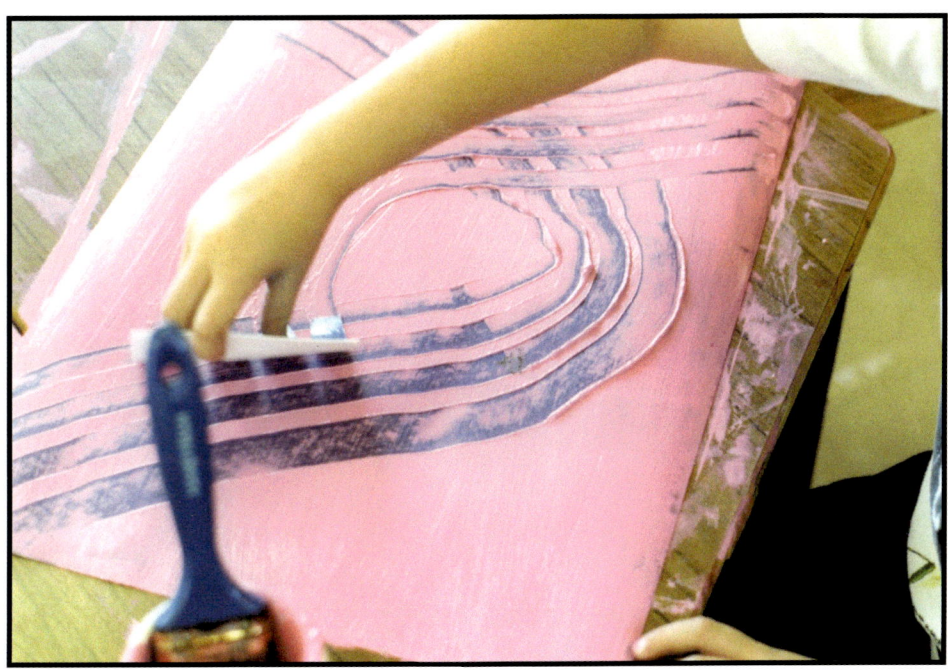

MrE's DEMONSTRATION

His demonstration of a possible background using a comb was too varied in colour and pattern. It was far too elaborate a background and yet at the same time did not seem to be a completed painting. What was he to do? He decided to ask the children for advice.

"You could splash or brush another colour over it so that it streaks across the page," suggested Melissa.

"That would be taking a risk or two. It might not work," replied their teacher.

"Come on MrE, be brave. Have a go. That's what you tell us to do."

"I know what you can do," said Julian, "Brush another colour over the top it and then you can use a comb to scratch patterns over it. Don't overdo it MrE."

"Thanks for your excellent suggestions. You have been a great help," the teacher assured them.

After some further attention MrE's demonstration ended up looking like this.

The children understood the problem. Many had faced a similar dilemma themselves. There was a touching empathy between the teacher and the children in his care. We were all learners and explorers working together and each of us were sometimes in the need of supportive advice. Decisions had to be made and the children were aware of that. The teacher accepted Julian's advice. The children felt more confident in making their own choices. It was wonderful that acrylic paints were so user friendly. Mistakes were easily fixed by covering them with fresh paint before continuing with the painting.

MrE

Adam first painted a merging yellow, blue, and red background before covering it with black on the following day. Before the black paint had time to dry, he scratched a swirling pattern with a cardboard comb. He then built upon his spectacular background and the finished painting can be found in the gallery.

TWO FINE BACKGROUNDS

Brent so much liked his swirling patterns created by a cardboard comb, that he decided to leave his painting as it was. He then tried to recreate the green background before further detailing with yellow patterns.

SUPERIMPOSING DETAILS OVER BACKGROUNDS

Some children dropped dollops of paint with a spoon over their background before teasing out patterns with large flat headed nails or icy pole sticks. Icy pole sticks proved to be popular as they had a thicker end yet still could be twisted and turned as they teased out the desired patterns.

Some children applied their newly found skill tricks in interesting combinations. Some enthusiasts like MrE, over did it a little, but we soon learned not to apply too much paint or add too many patterns.

"Keep it simple," was a phrase we kept in mind.

It was a marvellous sight watching the delight and excitement as the children discovered the effects of their superimposed skill tricks. They were becoming more confident with their risk taking as they searched for further discoveries. Our painting was bringing us closer together, as we all had a share in the creative experience. Their self-esteem continued to grow, and a more positive attitude was showing signs of spreading across the curriculum.

Jessica showed a most effective use of a cardboard comb. Her background had been previously painted black, and combs were then scratched through dollops of thick acrylic paint. The textures of thick creamy paint provided a visual and tactile treat.

Emma chose not to have a background at all. She immediately applied dollops of acrylic paint with a spoon on to her white background. She then scratched out patterns with combs and icy pole sticks.

Emma 10

Jessica 11

Damien carefully teased out some starfish patterns over his background. He first chose a dark background over which was covered a mixture of orange and brown. Before it was dry, he scratched out patterns with a cardboard comb. Later he would have added further patterns by teasing out from dollops of paint dropped over his modified background.

Samantha added some teases and twirls to her background. Her completed work can be found in the gallery.

THE EXCITEMENT OF A DISCOVERY

MrE had recently experienced a discovery of his own and he told the children of a little accident in his backyard shed where he sometimes painted a picture or two. Like most sheds it housed bottles, boxes of memorabilia and leftovers from his last attempt at house renovating. As he was working on one of his acrylic landscapes, a tin of wood varnish fell from a shelf and spilled a "Niagara" all over his nearly completed painting. Before he let out a naughty one, he was astonished to find that the polyurethane varnish really enriched the colours in his painting. He brushed the spilt varnish evenly across his canvass and admired the enhanced colours in front of him.

"Hm! Next time," he thought," I shall try that at school with a more considered deliberation."

He felt ecstatic with his discovery. So back at school and with ego-filled confidence, he used a house paint brush to cover one of his demonstrations with polyurethane. The large brush was horizontally swept across the surface so that an even grain was maintained. Excited children soon followed by brushing the varnish over their own completed acrylic paintings. The effect was stunning. The brushes used, for this purpose only, were kept in a glass jar half filled with turpentine.

Sometime later, on a visit to the nearest High School, MrE was agreeably surprised to find that his recently discovered technique had been in common use for some time. It was not his discovery after all. However, that mattered little as it remained a discovery felt by him and the children in his care. We felt motivated by its energetic force. We sparkled with delight as we the explorers felt really motivated to proceed with future creative journeys into the unknown.

Our ideas seemed to flow from one to another before merging into an aesthetic sense of completeness.

In my time at Risdon Vale, I would have tried this approach with Abstract Acrylic paintings at least three times. By the time I left the school, I would have seen about a hundred of these abstract paintings. I would have photographed about fifty of them. The selection found in the gallery reflects the work of children across a wide range of abilities. Some children thought to be of low ability often produced outstanding work. Success meant so much to them and as they felt so much better within themselves and their behaviour markedly improved. The criteria for selection were not simply based according to notions of excellence from an adult's point of view.

A WALK IN THE GALLERY

Julian S 10

Adam V 11

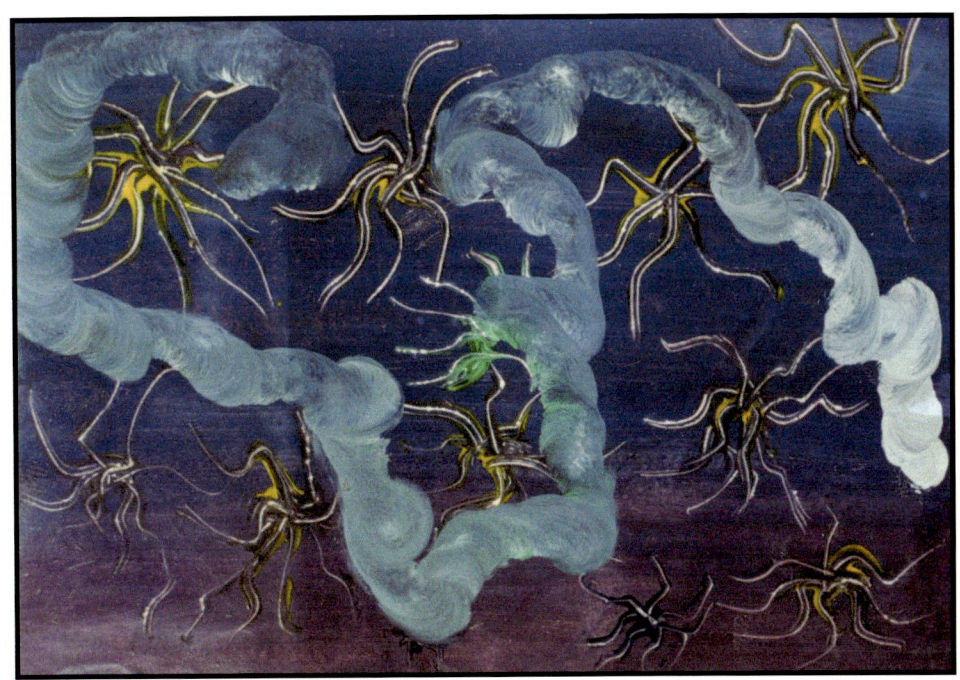

Amber D 11

Melissa J 10

Samantha T 11

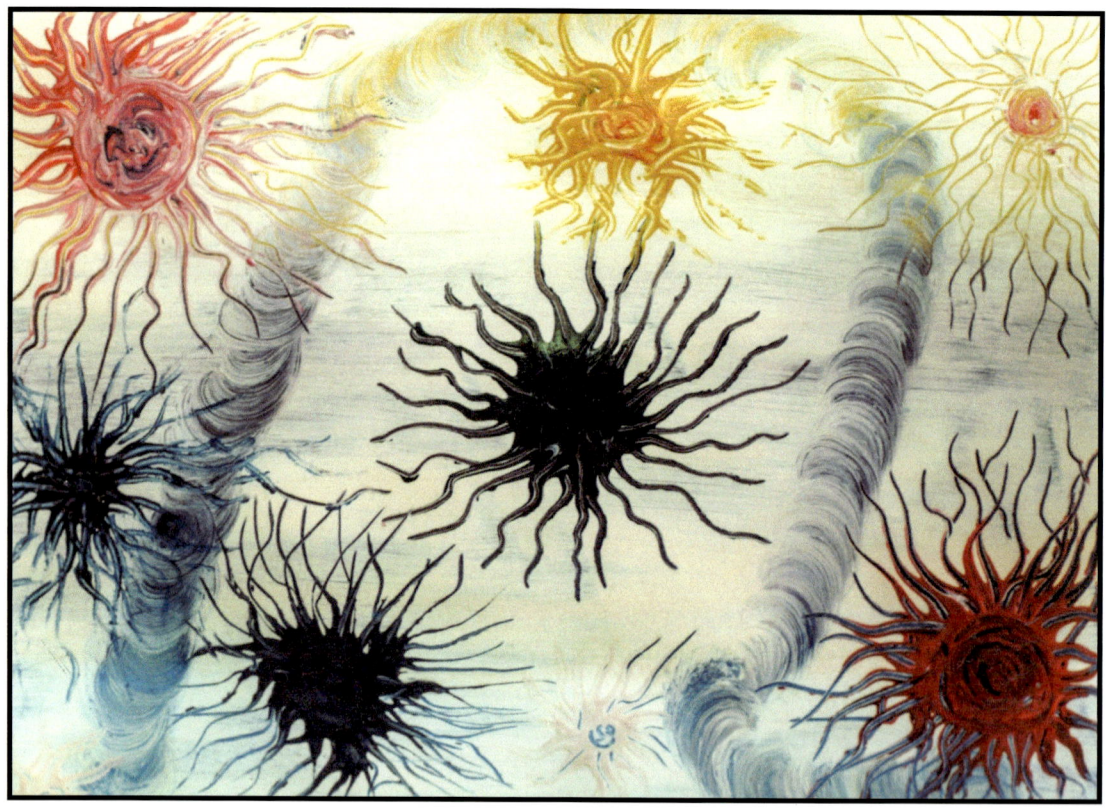

Danielle C 10

11 Clarissa M

Joshua P 11

Sarah L 11

Haylee O 11

Malinda B 10

Chris W 11

IN PRAISE OF COMPOSITE CLASSES

Whist I was the senior teacher at Taroona Primary school in the 1980's, I was persuaded by the principal to adopt the idea of working with composite classes. Instead of two grade fives and two grade sixes we adopted the use of four grade 5/6's. Gradually the idea was implemented throughout the school by making the year 3's and 4's functional as composite classes. There was some opposition at first from both teachers and parents. Some teachers believed that it would be too much work for them teaching two-year groups at a time. Some thought it affected the one-year programme that they had been using for years and that their workload would be doubled. Some teachers even thought that that their status was under threat. A grade six teacher thought she was top of the tree. Some parents thought that the older children in each composite class would be at a disadvantage by thinking their progress would be slowed down. So, I volunteered to be the guinea pig, after all it was nothing new, country, and small schools had used composite classes for years. I did however realise that was by necessity, and this innovation was by design.

I relished the challenge and enjoyed the prospect of teaching a group of children for two years. I worked out a series of programmes that developed over a period of two years. The activities within a programme naturally flowed from one to another. Over the years of my life as a teacher, the programmes evolved and were modified as my interests and experiences determined. Many of the improvements were suggested by the children themselves. They were an integral part of the flow. The units of creative works were constantly being modified depending on the needs and interests of the children and the time I had available to implement them. The creative units began with creative writing and soon spread into the world of 'ART'. I then designed creative units of work that encompassed the world of 'MATHEMATICS' and 'SCIENCE'.

The bands of composite classes were flexible enough to allow a child to be moved from one class to another at the end of each school year if there was good reason to do so. For my part, nearly all the children were happy to stay with me for the two years.

When you look at a unit of work and the amount of work involved in say, 'Painting Abstracts', one can be forgiven thinking "I can't do this! There is just too much work. Besides I've got a lot of other important work to do."

I was sympathetic to such views, but it must be realised that the activities were designed to be implemented over a period of two years. Think about it dear reader. I have already done the planning for you. All you need to do is find a starting point and off you go.

I nearly always treated the children in my composite class as a group. I did not see them as a group of grade 5 or 6 children. We worked together, sometimes alone but more often in small groups. Sometimes I worked with small groups according to their capabilities e.g.: with Number. In the main we pursued our creative explorations either as a class or with one small group at a time depending on the availability of space, time, and materials. Another advantage of composite classes was that some of the older children could be used as child tutors and be leaders of a creative activity with a small group of children. The children could always feel free to seek advice from each other or from their teacher if they found some of the challenges a little difficult. That often happened naturally as they worked in collaborative groups. I tried to avoid the word 'help'. To me, that implied someone might have wished for another to do the work for them. The children knew that they could opt out at times, if they felt out of reach with the task in hand, but that rarely happened. All the previous concerns held by teachers and parents were later proved to be unfounded. There was no doubt, the children and teachers had prospered.

When I took up my teaching post at Risdon Vale, I was pleased to discover that all the senior classes were composite year 5 /6. The children, the teacher realised, had come from rather different backgrounds with the school being the centre of a low socio-economic housing estate. So, he used Art to reach and teach the children in his care.

A TYPICAL DAY AT RISDON VALE

The day began with my arrival at school at 8-15 am and I arranged the materials needed for the day's activities. Some children drifted into the classroom after 8-30 am to continue with their previous explorations. By 8-55 am the whole class was ready for the day's action. We shall assume that on this day, we had no sessions organised by other staff members such as Phys Ed, Library, Music or Religious Instruction.

9 am Session 1

We began with a chat about what might happen during the day, and this was followed by some reading activities before numerical instruction with four separate groups. On Thursdays and Fridays, we would have worked together pursuing a practical mathematical exploration.

10-40 am RECESS

11 am Session 2

This time was given for the setting up of activities. It could have been 'Creative Writing', Historical Research or even the writing of short stories to share with some of the younger children in our school. The session may well have ended by the teacher reading a short story or part of a serialised novel to the children.

12 – 50pm LUNCH

1-30 Session 3

The afternoon sessions were often challenging and busy as the children enjoyed practical explorations. Some of these were of a mathematical nature. In small groups they might have explored the magical strength of paper. The teacher might have set up a new practical challenge whereby groups of two or three would try and solve the problem of making e.g.: Balloon powered cars with restricted available materials, such as a shoe box, wooden meat skewers, drinking straws, and a balloon. The teacher might have set up an artistic exploration e.g.: The drawing and painting of trees.

These busy sessions took place in the classroom, activity room, in the school playground and sometimes within the local community. Hopefully, we had enough time to clean up our workspaces before we were interrupted by the home time bell at 3 pm. Then the welcome peace was golden as the teacher made note of the day's highlights in his photographic journal.

MIXING POWDER PAINTS 1

Primary Colour Tones

Colour is a vibrant part of the world around us. If we try to paint the colours that we see, it follows that the mixing of colours to approximate the desired tones is an acquired skill of significance. It is amazing that most of the colours we need to paint can be mixed with yellow, blue, or red paint. We call these colours PRIMARY COLOURS. All that is needed are a few simple guidelines that we can follow, practice and revisit from time to time. We shall call these guidelines 'SKILL TRICKS' and they are challenging and fun to do.

   The children were asked to create as many tones as possible of the three primary colours. The tones could be varied by the amount of water held in the bristle brush or by the quantity of paint on the brush. Further specks of other primary colours could have been added to the mix. Some might have been tempted to add a speck or two of black and white.

   The children were challenged to make a COLOUR LINE on a provided worksheet designed by their teacher. They were asked to begin by painting a standard tone of their chosen primary colour in the centre of the worksheet. Thereafter, they could paint lighter or darker tones each side of it. When finished, one would hope to see a sheet showing a gradual progression of colour tone from 'light' on the left to a dark tone of the colour on the right. The children were strongly advised to have a testing sheet nearby to ensure their mix would be correctly placed on their worksheet. Some children tried all three of the primary colours. Some were happy to have just completed only one.

Adam is adding a light tone of yellow.

Julian is painting his last dark tone of red.

THREE EXAMPLES OF PRIMARY COLOUR LINES

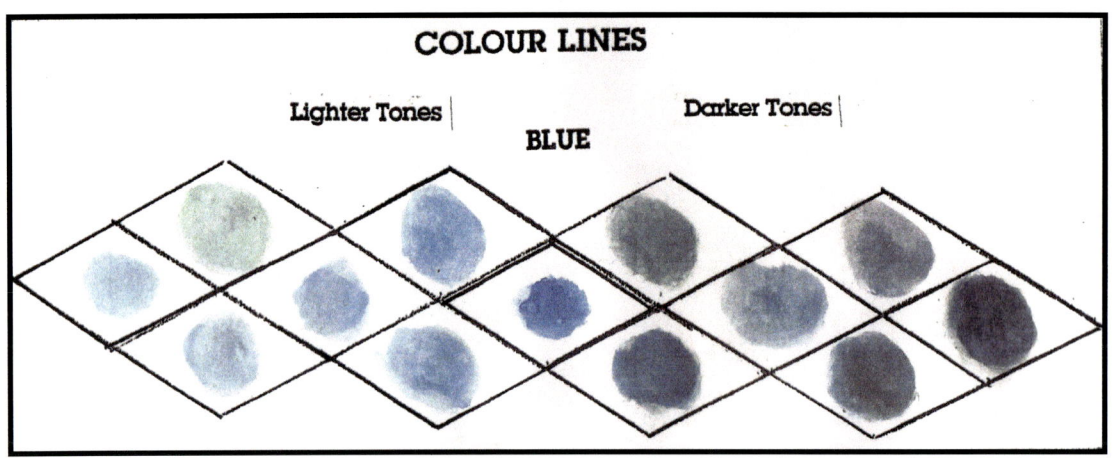

How might a little yellow or red vary the tones of 'blue'.

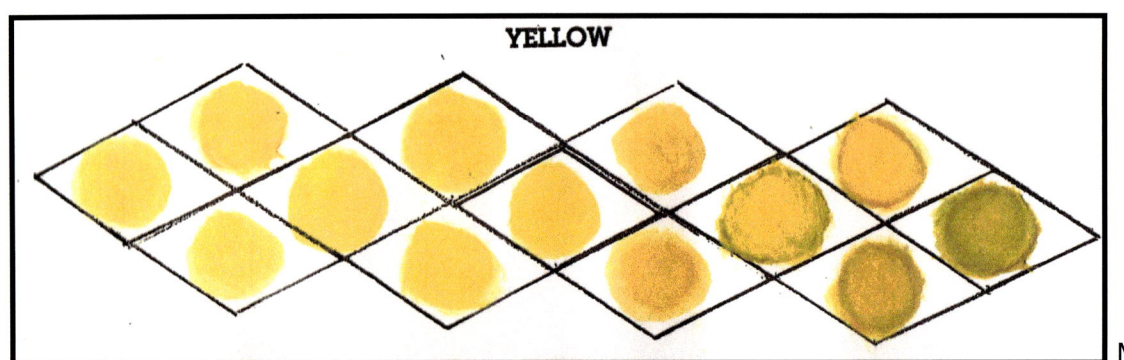

How might a little red or blue vary the tones of 'yellow'.

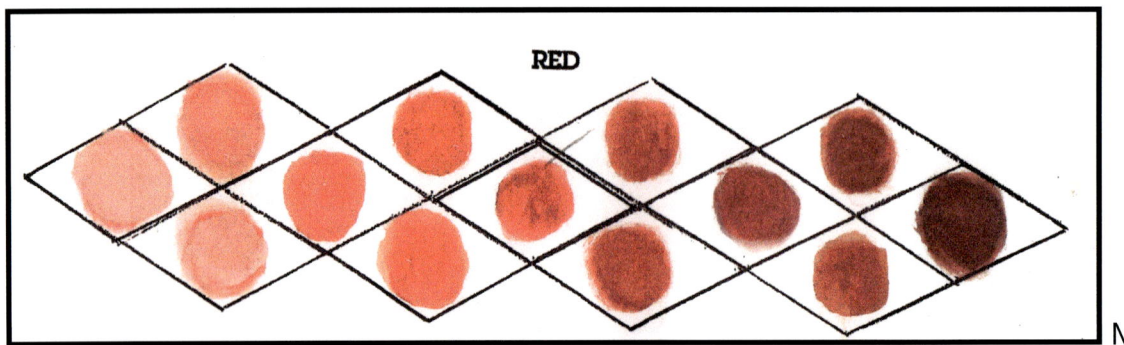

How might a little yellow or blue vary the tones of 'red'.

TOWARDS OUR FIRST LANDSCAPES

Our First Look at Trees

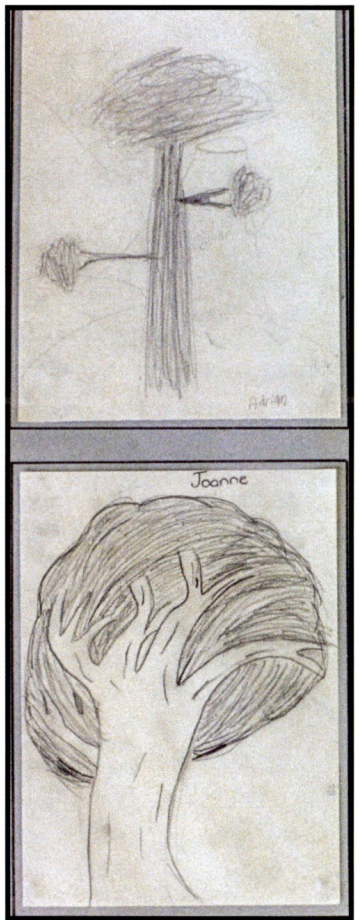

Adrian D + Joanna F

"Now children, I would very much like you to draw or paint a tree?"

"I am not very good at trees," said Brent.

"I'm hopeless at trees," mumbled Kaycee.

"Now where is all this negative talk coming from," replied their teacher. "It's OK, I know you might not be very good at drawing or painting a tree. I am just wishing to see your trees as you think they might look from your point of view. You are ten or eleven years old. I am not expecting to see an adult's view. I want to see a young person's view so I know where you are at and so that I might find a starting point for our new adventure."

They were by then at ease and were willing to try.

As expected, the children provided a variety of childlike drawings and paintings of trees. A few samples showed trees as Lollipops, that is a large green ball of foliage sitting on top of a basic brown tree trunk. Some were more elaborate and displayed branches striking out from trunks at strange looking angles with added clusters of green foliage.

It was a beginning and provided Mr E with his starting point. He decided to show them how they could draw a tree using a method that was within reach of their capabilities.

Louanne G + Luke C

Joanne F

Trent B

Louanne G

A LOOK AT TREES

DRAWING TREES

MATERIALS NEEDED

Pencils HB, 4V, or 6B
Cartridge Paper A4 Size
Erasers Rubber (Do not use Wipe Out)

MrE's DEMONSTRATION

STAGE 1

A gradually thinning tree trunk was drawn leaving spaces for two or three branches on either side of the trunk.

"Your branches should be growing upwards and gradually thinning out before splitting into two more thinning branches," explained their teacher.

"As your tree trunk gradually thins out towards the top it splits into two branches. Now see if you can follow these guidelines to start your own tree. Don't worry if you make a mistake, just erase it gently and carry on."

Stage 1

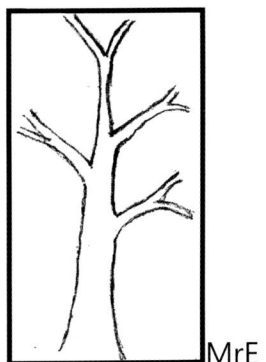

Stage 2

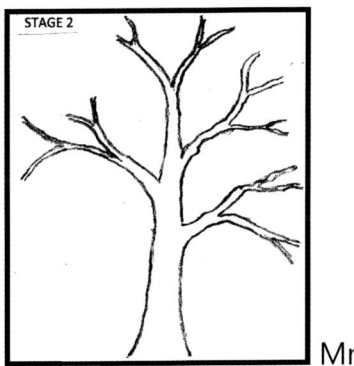

STAGE 2

"That's good. Well done, they look pretty good."

"Mine looks a little different than yours MrE," suggested Danielle.

"That's fine. You have drawn a couple more branches that's all. No trees in a forest look exactly alike, do they? As long as your trunk and branches appear to keep thinning."

The teacher now added a few developments to his first stage. Just after the first split of the branches he continued with each smaller branch, gradually thinning until that too was split into two smaller branches. The same procedure followed with the remaining branches.

"You can see by now the branches have become quite thin," said MrE.

"Yeah! They are looking more like twigs," added Melissa.

The children were then invited to add stage two to their first stage drawing of a tree. It was not often that MrE had all the children engaged in the same activity, so he was kept very busy providing encouragement and advice to all the children. They were applying themselves well and they had understood clearly what was asked of them.

STAGE 3

Following further from the thinning of branches, they were then further split into two or three super thin branches that again split into some pencil thin twigs at its extremity.

Stage 3

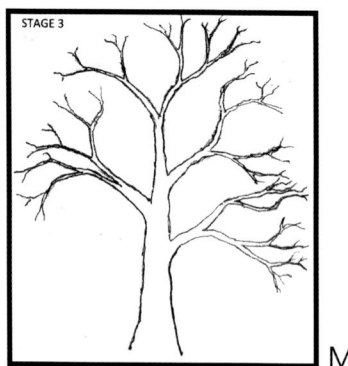

MrE

Stage 4

MrE

STAGE 4

The children were then showed how to add foliage to the branches. Clustered patches were shaded over and around the outer extremities of the thinning branches. The side of a soft pencil's lead tip moved backwards and forwards with short strokes suggested images of foliage.

"Hold the soft pencil lightly in your hand about a third of the way up the pencil. I am using a 6B pencil here to add some darker patches. Hopefully, this might help to create a sense of light and shade," as Mr E tried to explain during his demonstration.

"You can complete your drawing by gently shading parts of the tree trunk. If you shade too much of it, you can simply erase some of the excess shading by gently using a rubber. It might be a good idea to practice shading your clusters of leaves on a piece of testing paper first."

The children confidently proceeded the finishing touches of their drawing of an imaginary tree.

MrE is demonstrating his technique for the shading of clusters of leaves with a super soft 6b pencil.

"Now remember, we are not drawing individual leaves for that would take us a lifetime," he would say. "Each bit of shading gives an impression of a cluster of leaves."

The use of 2b and 6B pencils proved to be an excellent idea. Their use really helped us to create the difference between a dark and light shade.

They loved comparing their first efforts at the beginning of our explorative journey with their most recent efforts. They were amazed with the differences. Above all, they were so pleased with themselves and their achievements.

"It's a wonder what a few guidelines can do isn't it?" asked their teacher.

"It sure is Mr E. It makes us feel really good," added Josh.

Their teacher was quietly amazed as well. By tasting a glowing success with their drawing of trees, their self-esteem was given a huge boost. We have only just begun our journey into Landscapes; where to, might this journey lead us?

Damien thought he would like to try to draw another tree. Several children were so impressed with their drawings that they tried a second or even a third.

Megan W + Matt B

A CONVERSATION WITH MATT

"My tree trunk doesn't look right. I've shaded it in and rubbed it with my fingers and it still doesn't look right. What can I do MrE?"

"First you have to decide from which direction the light is coming from," suggested his teacher.

"I think it's coming from the right side," said Matt.

"Ok, I think the trunk will appear to be lighter on the side the sunlight is coming from don't you think?"

"Yes, I see that MrE, but what can I do about it?" asked Matt who was showing a few signs of frustration.

"Try using your rubber to gently shade out some of your tree trunk on the right side," suggested his teacher. "In the places where there are only dark shady areas, try a heavier shade by using a 6B pencil."

With confidence renewed, Matt set about adjusting the shading of his tree. A few minutes later he was back to show his rejuvenated tree to his teacher.

"You must be happy with that Matt. That's one of the best shaded trees that I have seen in years," remarked his teacher.

Matt B 10

A FOREST OF TREES

Kaycee J 10

TRY 1   TRY 2

A FOREST OF TREES

Jamie G 10

Luke S 10

Chris W 11

Julian S 10

Cade M 11

Danielle C 11

A Closer Look at Tree Trunks

The teacher decided it was time to look more closely at the shape, pattern, colours and texture of tree trunks. The perimeter of the school playground was endowed with a few Gum trees. The children set up their tables and chairs around a couple of chosen tree trunks. Our attention was to be focused on the lower three meters or at the point where the branches were beginning to emerge from the tree trunk.

MrE had made several view finders. These were rectangular pieces cut from stiff white cardboard about 16 by 13 cm. Inside that piece of cardboard a further rectangle was drawn about 10 by 7 cm before that too was cut out. When the piece of cardboard was held at a little distance from your face you could focus on your subject through the space created by the cut-out centre piece. This helped us to concentrate on a particular subject area.

"What you see through your view finder, should correspond with the sheet of paper upon which your subject will be drawn," said MrE.

The children were encouraged to draw, with 6B pencils, what they actually saw through their view finders pointing at the chosen subject. The rubbing of fingers and thumbs over pencil shades enabled effective variations of tone.

This tree proved very popular as you can judge by the number of chairs and tables that surrounded it. The children are seen to be using their view finders to focus on the relevant part of the tree trunk. The colourful patterns of the trunk are quite striking to the eye, particularly after a recent fall of rain. If some of the bark had recently been shed the rain really enriched the colours of the trunk.

The children in the main sat in pairs to facilitate supportive conversation. Here we see Joshua pointing out to Luke a particular feature of his interest in the coloured patterns of the tree trunk.

Another feature of our tree experience in the playground was the feeling of the tree trunks with our fingers. Some parts of a trunk had a very rough feel, others were found to be so soft and smooth to the touch.

Danielle is feeling her way around the tree trunk. This should help her appreciation of the trunk's texture.

"If we put on our Ned Kelly hat our sense of touch might be further heightened," suggested MrE.

"If we take one of our senses away for a while the other senses seem to work harder," he continued.

The idea of texture was within their grasp.

A Ned Kelly hat is simply made by rolling a sheet of black cover paper into a cylindrical shape so that it rests on the shoulders. Thus, the wearer would be unable to see.

"I wonder how we could show the texture of these trees in our drawings?" asked the teacher.

"I reckon we could make the bark look rough with a very soft pencil like a 6B," answered Danielle.

"I think we should try and paint some tree trunks using some really thick paint," suggested Joshua.

David gently holds his soft pencil as he shades the varied texture of bark.

Julian S 10

Cade M 11

PAINTING TREE TRUNKS

It had been raining during the morning but by lunch time the rain had passed us by, and the playground was bathed in sunshine. The teacher suggested that the children see the effect of the sunlight on the tree trunks after the recent rain. He was on playground duty during the lunch break so he could watch from a distance if any children showed any interest in the tree trunks. He was so pleased to see half a dozen children observing the trunk of our favoured tree. Two of them were Chris and Cade who were in fact showing some boys from another class some interesting features of the tree.

After lunch I praised the children for showing such interest and invited them to paint a picture of the tree trunk.

First, they drew a faint outline of the tree trunk and its patterns on cartridge paper. They then applied powder paint to recreate the soft coloured patterns of the tree trunk.

Cade added the finishing touch to his painted tree trunk. Chris and Cade had inspired other children to follow.

Cade M 11

Chris W 11

TIME FOR A SKILL TRICK OR TWO

1 Rolling Bristle Brushes

Before we completed our first journey into the wonderful world of Landscapes, it was fitting to experiment with a couple more Skill Tricks.

A bristle brush was dipped into a container of water and was then gently squeezed between the fingers. The moistened brush was then flatly rolled across a mixture of powder paint before it was rolled across a piece of paper. Notice how the children are holding their brushes. They are holding them way up the handle and keeping the brush as low as possible to have as much of the side of the brush touching the paper as possible.

Children were encouraged to experiment with drier brushes and some that were quite wet. Some children then experimented using a variety of bristle brush sizes and types e.g.: Round or Flat. This technique later proved to be useful in simulating the images of Grasses, rushes or even shrubs over simple landscape backgrounds.

"As the bristle brush is collecting powder paint remember to ensure that the side of the brush is fully covered with paint before it is rolled across the cartridge paper," said MrE.

This popular skill trick was especially effective when rolling, moist to wet brushes coated with powder paint, across the sheet of cartridge paper.

These two examples of a record sheet clearly show the effects of rolling bristle brushes. Try and identify which rolling brushes were used with dry, moist, or wet brushes.

MrE then suggested, "Display some of your record sheets on the classroom wall. They might provide us with a handy reference when we try our first Landscapes."

2 DABBING BRISTLE BRUSHES

Moist bristle brushes were dipped in powder paint before their tips were lightly dabbed on paper. The children experimented by using a variety of bristle brushes with round or flat tips. They also varied the amount of moisture in the brushes.

The children were then encouraged to build up a chart that showed each variable cluster of dabs. For each cluster they provided an appropriate label.

Brent is dabbing a few clusters showing a variety of orange tones.

The children were frequently reminded to apply only a gentle pressure when dabbing their brushes and to keep their brushes moist rather than wet.

Here we see two girls building up their colour chart.

"Hey Ho, Hey Ho, a dabbing we will go," Mr E sang, as he walked around the room soon to be joined by a chorus of children.

This is a colour chart that is near completion. On this sheet we see the use of small and large round bristle brushes. The differences between the use of dry, moist, and wet brushes are clearly visible.

PAINTING TREES

The children were asked to faintly draw the outline of a tree trunk with thinning branches.

"Try to remember that the trunk and branches gradually thin towards the outer reaches of the tree," suggested their teacher. "This time, there is no need to shade the trunk and branches or shade the cluster of leaves. Your paint brushes will later add the details," he continued.

"Are you going to do one MrE?" asked Mitchell.

"Yes, I will draw one and then I'll be able to demonstrate the next stage,"

He later gave a brief demonstration of the use of soft haired brushes and small bristle brushes showing how the tree trunks and branches were textured with patches of mixed powder paints. The children then proceeded with the painting of their own trees. Their recent experience with tree trunks certainly helped them apply the subtle colour variations of the trunk and major branches.

Small bristle brushes were handy for painting the thicker part of the tree trunk but as the trunk and branches thinned out, it was easier to paint smaller details with the tips of soft haired brushes.

"It is a good idea to wet your soft-haired brush first and then use your fingers to make a thin tip. I also like to use a bristle brush for mixing my colours before I use the soft-haired brush to add my details," MrE told the children during his demonstration.

"Now you can paint your trunk and branches first and then I'll show you how we can add clusters of leaves," he added.

The children then painted their tree trunks and branches. It was stressed that the brushes should only be moist when they added their mix of powder paint. There soon appeared some lovely colour mixes for their trunks and branches. Recent experiences with colour mixing had served them well.

ADDING FOLIAGE

It was now time to demonstrate the painting of foliage. The teacher showed them the dabbing of damp medium round bristle brush coated with yellowy to dark greens in patchy clusters over and around the thinning branches. Some testing paper nearby would prove to be a useful safeguard to maintain the correct amount of moisture in the brush. The testing also helped us to maintain the desired mixture of coloured powder paint. A mixture of shades was encouraged to facilitate the variation of light and colour.

"Is that why we did some dabbing a couple of weeks ago"? asked Chris.

"Yes, you are right Chris. However, try not to overdo it with your dabbing. Leave some spaces between your clusters so that light could be seen to shine through the foliage," said Mr E.

This photograph of a tree in our playground clearly suggests that dabbing clusters of paint with tips of medium to large bristle brushes is so appropriate for capturing the image of foliage.

The children had recently been shown how to roll moistened bristle brushes coated with powder paint across a sheet of paper to create the appearance of grasses.

"Just remember to hold the brush in both hands and use your thumb and forefinger to roll your brush across the base of the tree," suggested the teacher.

"Try to keep your large and medium bristle brushes nice and moist before you add the paint and also remember to trial a roll or two on testing paper first," he added.

One must acknowledge that our trees looked rather stylised and two dimensional. That's fine with me as they are only our first serious attempts, and we are early in our journey towards a world of landscapes.

However, he did make the point, "Do you think that our trees look a little flat?" asked Mr. E of a small group of painters.

"You mean they don't look round," Haylee remarked.

"Yes, it looks as if we can't walk around them like we did the other day." added Joshua.

"If ever we were to paint another tree, I wonder what we could do to make them look a little more three dimensional," suggested MrE. He left them with that food for thought.

ADDING A SKILL TRICK

A FOREST OF PAINTED TREES

Matt B 10

Kristy A 10

Joshua P 11

Mitchell B 10

Dannielle C 11

Malinda B 11

Jessica W 10

Haylee O 11

Chris S 10

Luke C 10

Nicole A 11

Matt B 11

A CLASSROOM DISPLAY

Some children wished to display all three stages of their tree drawings and paintings. They clearly illustrated how far we have travelled on this artistic journey towards our first landscapes. We had a splendid view from this milestone and the explorers looked forward to the journey ahead.

MIXING POWDER PAINTS 2

UNDERSTANDING THE COLOUR WHEEL

MATERIALS NEEDED

Powder Paints Red, Blue, and Yellow
Small soft hairbrushes, Large soft hairbrushes
Paint containers and Paint mixing trays
Plastic teaspoons
Blank pad paper for Testing
A ruler and pencil, A compass and Protractor

A simple colour wheel with three primary colours

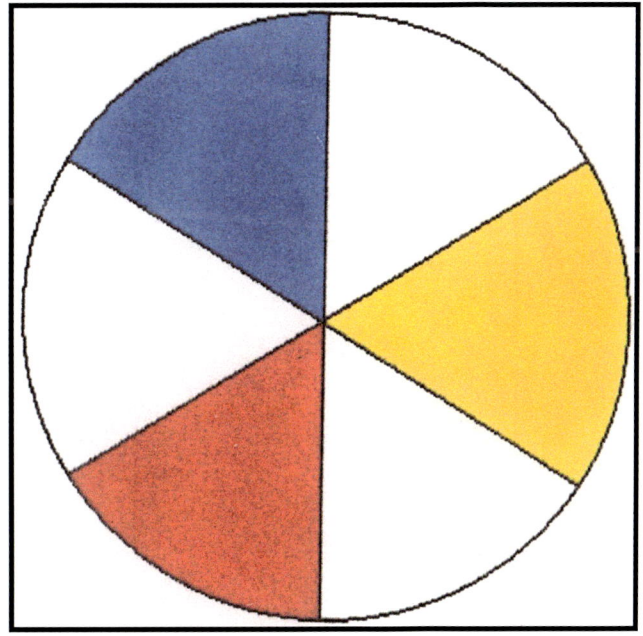

MAKING OUR OWN COLOUR WHEELS

The children were asked to construct a circle with six equal segments. It would be great if they could do so by themselves by using a compass and a protractor. First, they would have ruled a diameter through the centre of the circle from north to south. They would have then followed by measuring angles of 60 degrees from the centre of the circle and marking the spot on the circumference. They continued until six equal segments had been created within the circle. The children painted a different primary colour in every second segment. Then they mixed two primary colours in equal portions and painted them in the segment between the two primary colours. We call the resulting colours, Purple, Orange, and Green, Secondary Colours. Many tones of Secondary Colours can be made by mixing varying amounts of the neighbouring primary colours.

Sarah is completing her colour wheel by adding a mix of red and yellow to create the secondary colour 'ORANGE'

A COMPLETED SIMPLE COLOUR WHEEL

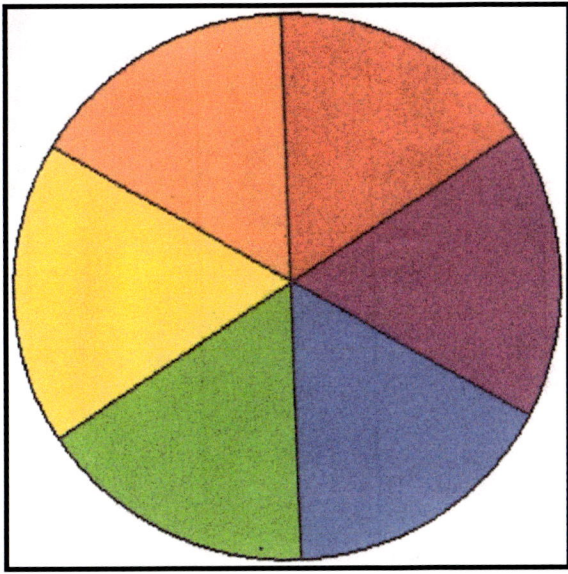

In this simple colour wheel, we have three primary colours each neighboured by a secondary colour. It should have been noticed that each neighbouring pair of primary and secondary colours softly blended.

"I wonder what might happen if we mixed two neighbouring colours together?" suggested MrE. "For example, if we mixed purple with blue or green with yellow."

"I wonder what would happen if we mixed all six together?" suggested Julian.

The teacher felt they were moving ahead of his intended agenda. However, he gave the rope some slack and for the moment he drifted with the flow. So, the colour wheel became a temporary spinning wheel. It seemed that with a good spin the secondary colours merged with the primary colours. It was interesting to note that only the primary colours could be clearly visible.

Just for a fleeting moment MrE was hoping to see a blurry brown. Alas, Julian could not spin the colour wheel fast enough.

"I wonder what would happen if we mixed all the colours of the rainbow?" asked Lisa.

With his answer MrE hopefully posed, "I wonder what would happen if we just mixed two neighbouring colours on the colour wheel.

HARMONY AND CONTRAST IN COLOUR

Colour wheels helped us understand more about colours and how they reacted with each other. Neighbouring colours on the colour wheel softly blended as they sat side by side

."They sing together in harmony. If we place together two colours that stand opposite to each other on the colour wheel they are in contrast with each other. They help each other to stand up and be noticed. They are not related to each other," explained their teacher.

"Now, choose a primary colour and harmonise it by surrounding it with its two-neighbouring secondary colours. Then compare the effect on the primary colour when it is surrounded by a contrasting colour.

Yellow is in harmony with Orange and Green

Yellow is in contrast with Purple

Let us see what happens when a secondary colour is surrounded by the Primary colours.
In these two examples we see those green blends harmoniously with yellow and then with blue. Green is made by the mixing of blue and yellow. They are related.

Here we see that Green is in contrast with red. Red stands opposite to Green in the colour wheel. This combination helps the Green to stand out. Those are two contrasting colours and they are not related.

PAINTING COLOURS IN HARMONY AND CONTRAST

The children were provided with a sheet of cartridge paper upon which were drawn three circles of a diameter 4cm. Each circle was surrounded by a boundary that suggested three fried eggs.

Emma was painting the contrasting purple around the primary colour yellow.

Here we see that both blue and red are surrounded by harmonious colours.

The children painted the same primary colour in each of the small circles. The first two were surrounded by the two neighbouring colours in harmony. The third was surrounded by the colour opposite to it on the colour wheel. Thus, the third fried egg stood out in contrast.

Some children were encouraged to mix the paint powders together before adding any water. They would then add their damp brush to the mixed powders. They had never tried that before.

During the painting activities the children were encouraged to be sparing in their use of powder paint. After seeing some children literally tipping tins of paint onto mixing trays, the general practice of using a teaspoonful at a time proved to be more than sufficient.

PAINTING PRIMARY COLOURS IN HARMONY AND CONTRAST WITH SECONDARY COLOURS

Blue in harmony with Purple and Green   Blue in contrast with Brown

Yellow in harmony with Green and Orange   Yellow in contrast with Purple

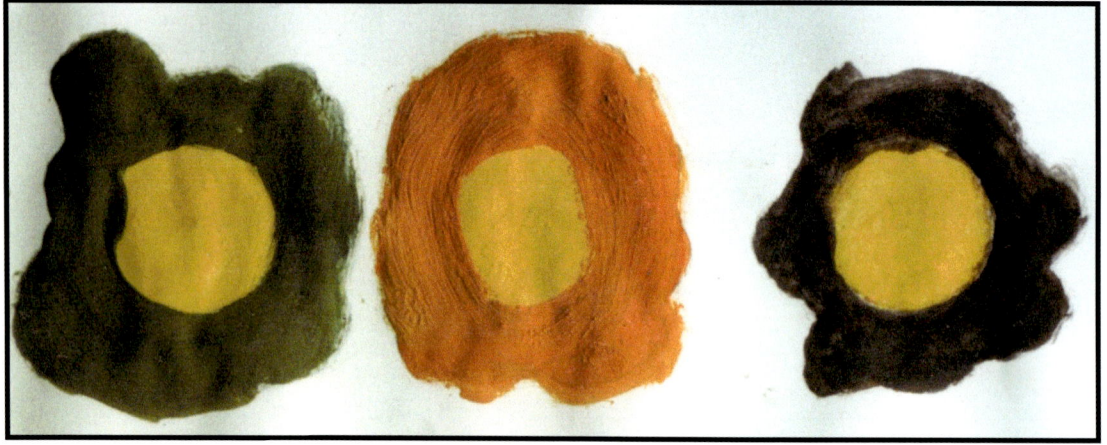

Red in Harmony   Red in Contrast

SECONDARY COLOURS

These colours have harmonious and contrasting partners too

Green in Harmony   Green in Contrast

Purple in Harmony   Purple in Contrast

Orange in Harmony   Orange in Contrast

OUR FIRST LANDSCAPES

MATERIALS NEEDED

POWDER PAINT .... teaspoons of Red, Blue, Yellow, White, and Black.
PAINT CONTAINERS and MIXING TRAYS.
PAINT BRUSHES .... Assorted Bristle Brushes, Soft Haired Brushes and a few Medium to large House paint Brushes.
PAPER.... Sheets of A3 sized Cartridge paper and a sheet of blank pad paper for testing colour mixes. PENCILS.... HB for drawing faint outlines.

After the successful drawing and painting of imaginary trees, it was time for us to plant a tree or two in an imaginary landscape.

The teacher preferred to work with a group of about six to eight children at a time, at trapezoidal desks in the classroom or by standing at large tables in the activity room. He first set about ensuring that the rest of the class had plenty to do, so that he could spend a few minutes with the Landscape group.

"What happens if they play up while you are out of the room?" asked my student teacher.

"I doubt that they will. They just know that they might not be invited to join the next group for landscapes," replied MrE.

PRELIMINARY SKETCHES

STAGE 1

BACKGROUND SKETCHES

The teacher demonstrated the drawing of the major outlines of his imaginary landscape.

THE SKYLINE .... Where the sky met the distant hills.

"As you can see, I am first drawing a hill from the right side of my paper from about two thirds up the sheet of paper. It flattens out into the middle ground of the picture which is about two thirds across the paper. From the left side I am drawing the outline of a distant hill that meets the hill that I have already drawn."

The teacher suggested that they could if they wished, add a third distant hill between the two already drawn.

"It would be easier for you to keep it all simple, ok?"

STAGE 2

MIDDLE GROUND

Where the distant hills meet the plain
The teacher drew a faint line across the sheet from the base of the nearest hill.
"You can add a distant tree if you wish," suggested MrE.

STAGE 3

FOREGROUND

This is the space and places that are nearer to us.
Their teacher suggested that they might like to add the outlines of a river, road, or pond.
"Remember, if you want to draw a road or a river they must seem to lead somewhere and that they appear to narrow as they reach into the picture's distance. You can start your own outlines now but be sure to keep your outlines faint. I'll be back in a few minutes."
The teacher returned his attention to the rest of the class to check on their progress with the designing and making of 'Super Gliders'. A few minutes later he returned to the group of Landscapers.
"How are we all going?" he asked.
"I'm finding that my road is too hard MrE," replied Trent.

"My pond looks a bit funny," added Samantha.

"Now let's have a look," answered their teacher. I see, I think Trent that you can leave it out or watch a little demonstration to show you what it could look like. What would you prefer?"

"I think I'll carefully rub it out."

"Very well; now Samantha, I think your pond is going to look fine. I'll show you how to add some painted details later."

The questions and answers continued to flow.

Some preliminary outlines may have looked like this.

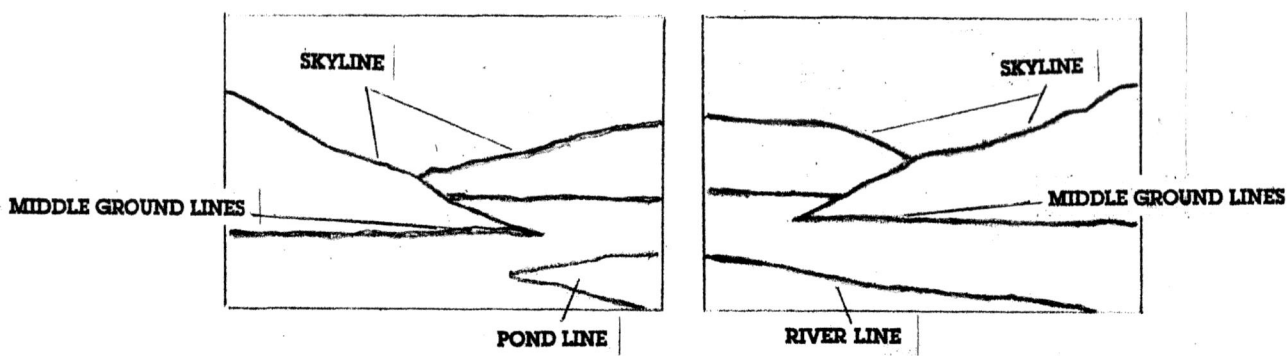

These preliminary outlines have been accentuated. The original outlines on cartridge paper would have been too faint to be seen.

STAGE 4

A LARGE FOREGROUND TREE

MrE retrieved his earlier demonstration of outlines for a landscape painting and began drawing an outline of a large tree over the top of his previous outlines. He did this with an audience of about six children.

"Just draw a similar tree to the one you drew last week. Start your tree a little way up from the bottom of the sheet but make the top of the upper branches break into and above the skyline like this. If you draw the tree on one half of the sheet it might leave room for something else a little later. This time, just draw the outline as there is no need for shading trunks and branches or drawing thin twigs.

"I know, the paint brush will do the rest," added a cheeky Julian.

A few minutes later, the teacher returned to find that their added trees were well placed and drawn.

"Well done everyone. We shall start adding paint in a few days' time."

"Why not now!" they exclaimed.

"Because I now hope you will do a special job for me. I would like each one of you to find a friend and show him or her what I have already shown you. Would you like to be a special teacher for a little while?"

They all agreed to play the role of acting tutors. Within five minutes they had found a willing friend and had begun their demonstrations. It 'snowballed' from there and by the end of the afternoon more than half the class had completed the outlines of their landscape and had superimposed a large tree. The tutors closely followed the teacher's style of demonstration. It was a joy for the teacher to watch the discourse between child tutor and child from a safe distance. They even remembered to avoid touching their pupil's drawing paper. They demonstrated each part by referring to their own outlines or by showing them on a separate piece of paper. MrE liked that, as the learners retained the ownership of their own drawings. By the following afternoon everyone had completed the outlines of their first landscape.

PAINTING OUR FIRST LANDSCAPES

STAGE 1 SKY WASHES

A medium to large round bristle brush, lightly tipped with powder paint of a chosen sky colour was left at the ready. Light blues and greys were popular choices. The teacher was ready for his demonstration.

His wet house paint brush was quickly brushed across the paper above the skyline. He used quick and broad left to right movements to evenly wet the paper. Then he quickly took hold of his round bristle brush dipped in powder paint and lightly brushed it in patches across the sky space. The clear spaces were left for later consideration. It was all over in less than a minute.

"You can see how quickly this is done," he said. "I'm pleased that my house paint brush did not create any wrinkled valleys as that might have made it difficult to paint the patches of blue or grey sky. If your paper does become wrinkled simply wipe the house paint brush dry and use the brush to soak up the excess water. The secret is to be a little sparing in your use of water. Now I'll stand back and watch you have a go."

The small group dutifully adopted their teacher's instructions. First, they applied powder paint to their bristle brushes and followed that by carefully adding water to their large house paint brush.

"Is that the right amount of water MrE?" an uncertain voice enquired.

"I'm not sure but be quick to brush it across your sky space," he replied.

"Now quickly use your bristle brush already dipped in paint," he added. "There you are, it's done. Well, done."

"Oh No! I've got valleys in my sky," came the anguished cry from Blair.

A 3 CARTRIDGE PAPER

The quality of cartridge paper has deteriorated over the years of my teaching experience. It is not as thick and absorbent as it used to be. These days when a house paint brush soaked with water is brushed along a sheet of paper it sometimes becomes warped with wrinkles. This causes the paint to run in unwanted directions.

"Keep your brush wet rather than saturated."

This photograph clearly illustrates the problem with over watered washes. Some children found it useful to use masking tape to stretch and affix the sheet of cartridge paper onto a slightly elevated board. Sometimes, it might be a good idea to purchase good quality water colour paper.

"MrE, I asked for help," added a desperate Blair.

Quick as a flash, MrE took a clean tissue from his pocket and said, "Quickly mop it up with this." The painting was saved.

"Well done everybody. I think you can stop now. We don't need to paint the whole sky blue," was his gentle reminder.

"Phew! That was scary," said Haylee. "I kept thinking I was going to mess it up."

"I was really nervous MrE, but I'm glad we got through it OK." added Mitchell.

"That's quite alright to feel uneasy when you try something new. Art does that to us sometimes. Just think of when you were first riding a two-wheeler bike; I bet you felt nervous and worried about falling off. You soon got used to it, didn't you? It's the same with painting. The idea of "washes" is new to you. You have a little challenge to overcome. Soon it will be so much easier for you. Now would you like to show a friend how it's done?" asked MrE.

STAGE 2 MIDDLE AND FOREGROUND WASHES

The teacher would have preferred to demonstrate the use of washes with a small group of children at a time. Some of them could then be used as child tutors to work with a partner or two. If that was not possible the furniture of the activity room would have to be rearranged. A small demonstration table might be surrounded by chairs for some to sit whilst the remaining children stood behind the chairs.

The sky wash should be left to dry before painting the distant hills. If some children wished to continue straight away, they could have next applied a similar wash over their middle and foreground. This would have helped to prevent undesirable paint runs from the sky to the distant hills. The wash would have been followed by a light application of greens, browns, and yellows in left to right movements across the sheet of cartridge paper. The space for a pond, road or river could have been left clear during the middle and foreground washes.

STAGE 3 THE DISTANT HILLS

After the sky and middle ground washes had dried, the distant hills were only lightly washed before a gentle application of pale mauves and perhaps light bluey greys.

"If you look closely at the landscape outside you might notice that the sky is not all a bright blue on a sunny cloudless day," said MrE. "As you look towards the skyline, you might notice that the sky is a paler blue. It appears to be a darker blue the further you look up in the sky," he continued. "So, it is similar with the distant hills. We all know that hills closer to us are coloured with greens, browns, and yellows, but if you look to the hills on a distant horizon, you should see more paler colours. You might see soft pastel-coloured hills of mauve and perhaps bluey grey. Next time you are taken for a drive in the country take a closer look. You might be surprised by what you see."

STAGE 4 SUPERIMPOSING DETAIL

TREES

After our background was left to dry, we proceeded with the adding of details over the top of it. We then lightly sketched and painted a tree using our recently acquired techniques. The top of the tree would have broken the picture's skyline. Another tree was added to the middle ground so that we could reach and feel our way into the picture's distance.

"Remember that your trees appear to be smaller as you reach further towards the distant hills," remarked their teacher.

THE FINISHING TOUCHES

Our first landscapes were nearing a sense of completion. The children were applying their final details to their paintings. Some were adding clusters of foliage to their trees while a few of them were rolling bristle brushes around the base of their tree trunks.

"Do you think it's a good idea to add details over a previously painted background?" asked their teacher to a group of children sitting close by.

"Yes! I do. It's much better this way," added Blair.

"It's not so messy," suggested Haylee.

"Sometimes when my young children were painting at home, I noticed that they liked to paint the most important things first. Then they had a lot of problems trying to add the sky and foreground around them. It took me ages to persuade them to add the more important things last," said MrE.

"That's funny MrE, I used to do just that," said Nicole.

"Me too," added Matt.

"I probably did it as well when I was a young lad. It's funny how we change the way we do things as we become older. We are learning all the way through our lives, not just when we are working at school. I have learned a lot of things by working with you this year," said MrE.

"I thought you knew all about art and things MrE?"

"That's far from the truth, When I started teaching, I hardly knew anything about art. I've picked up a few ideas along the way and eventually worked out a suitable art programme like I have done for you. I am still learning and no doubt I shall learn more as I grow older."

"That's very interesting MrE. Will it be the same with us?"
"I'm sure it will be so," replied their teacher.

THE RIVER OR POND

MrE's DEMONSTRATION PAINTING A POND

A background of sky colours was first applied with a small bristle brush in gentle sweeping movements across the water space. Sometime later, darker tones were added near the distant banks to give a shady impression.

On the banks of the pond a moist bristle brush coated with yellow, and green was brushed in short left to right brush strokes.

A damp medium sized bristle brush thinly coated with specks of grey and black was very lightly dragged horizontally across the surface of the water space.

A moist round bristle brush dipped in a mix of greens, yellows and browns was rolled across the edge of the pond to create the effect of reeds and rushes

IN A NUTSHELL

1 SKYWASH

MrE

2 MIDDLEGROUND WASH

3 DISTANT HILLS AND FOREGROUND WASH

4 APPLYING DETAILS

PART OF A CLASSROOM DISPLAY

I firmly believed that our creative and explorative approach to learning ensured for us great pleasure and success. Most of the children were genuinely surprised by the beauty of their paintings. You could see and feel their confidences grow. They were ready to embrace the challenge of painting a landscape at a nearby location.

A WALK IN THE GALLERY

Julian S 10

Luke C 10

Mitchell B 10

Haylee O 10

Blair G 10

Samantha T 11

Cody C 11

Stefan T 10

Joshua P 11

Joanne F 11

Cassie D 11

Cade M 11

MIXING POWDER PAINTS 3

Expanding The Colour Wheel

By adding a rim to our colour wheel, we could show the development of further colours. We simply chose a Primary Colour e.g.: 'BLUE' and mixed with equal portion its neighbouring secondary colour, e.g.: 'GREEN' on a sheet of testing paper. We were richly rewarded with a 'DARK GREEN'. The dark green was then transferred to its appropriate spot on the rim of the expanded colour wheel. We continued by mixing similar pairs of colours and painting them on the rim until the expanded colour wheel is completed.

EXPANDED COLOUR WHEEL

WHEEL RIM

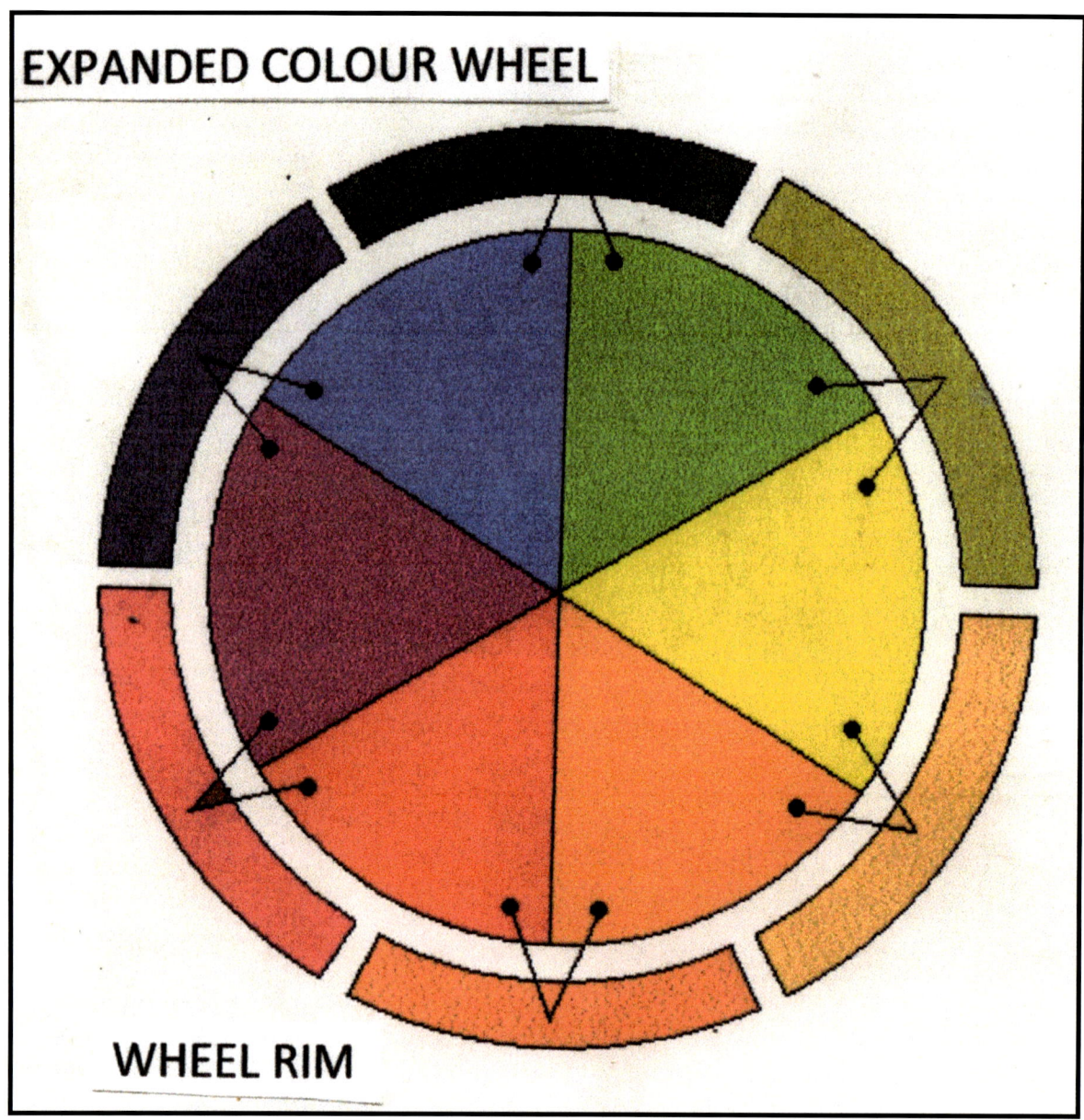

The children were delighted to discover some softer pastel colours and had fun finding names for some of them. Some recalled names like 'mauve" but some were cheeky enough to apply their own names for some of the colours, e.g.: SLME GREEN.

WHERE TO NEXT?

We could seek further variation of tones by mixing unequal portions of Primary and Secondary colours. We could have expanded the colour wheel even further by mixing each coloured pair on the rim to create an outer rim of colours. Instead, the teacher decided to test the Harmony and Contrast in the colours of the wheel rim.

SEEKING HARMONY AND CONTRAST IN COLOURS FROM THE RIM OF THE EXPANDED COLOUR WHEEL

The children chose a colour from the rim of the colour wheel e.g.: 'Dark Green'. The colour was painted in the centre of three fried egg shapes. The colour on either side of it on the rim e.g.: "Slime Green' or 'Mauve' was then painted in the yoke centre of the three fried egg shapes. We considered these colours to be in harmony. Around the third yoke centre, the colour opposite the chosen colour on the wheel rim e.g.: 'Pumpkin' or 'Dark Orange' was painted in to demonstrate an effective contrast. It was interesting for us to notice a greater degree of subtlety with the harmonies and contrasts with the chosen colours from the rim of the expanded colour wheel.

AN EXAMPLE

'Slime Green' the chosen colour, is painted in the centre of three fried eggs. On the outer rim of the first two eggs the two-neighbouring harmonious colours, 'Dark Green' and 'Pale Orange' were painted in. In the third egg the colour opposite 'Slime Green' which was 'Mauve' was painted in to create a pair of contrasting colours. In this example we might have to obtain an artist's license to identify the colour 'Mauve."

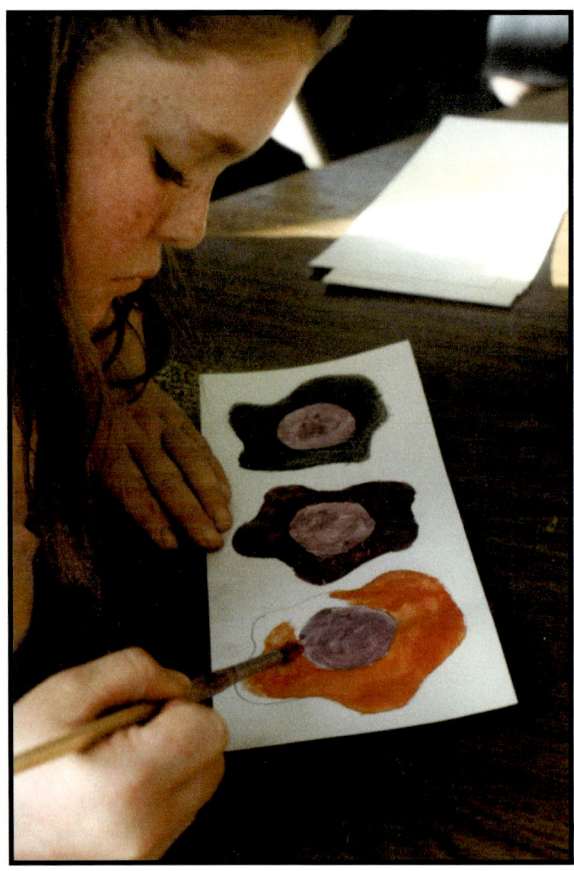

"OH NO! NOT FRIED EGGS AGAIN."

As the colours became more sophisticated in name and appearance a greater degree of subtlety was evident in their harmonious and contrasting relationships

Perhaps we could harvest this essence of subtlety and use it when we first paint our Landscapes.

"Just where do you get your ideas from?" asked Haylee.

"That is a question that is often asked of me. I would give them a smile and say,

"From those wonderful people who surround me."

BOOKS ABOUT ART AND ARTISTS

A SOURCE OF SUPPORT AND INSPIRATION

Our school librarian was aware of our interest in art, and she purchased some wonderful books about art and artists for the school. At this time of the year, these books found their way into our classroom for a week or two. The accompanying photographs show some children looking at the work of artists that showed an interesting use of colours in harmony and in contrast. Some of the books displayed the work of 19th and 20th century impressionists and using their colour wheels as a guide the children were quickly attracted to the works of Van Gough. Some of his paintings clearly demonstrated the power of contrasting colours. Likewise, they enjoyed the soft coloured harmonies that shone through the works of Monet.

MINI PAINTINGS BY JUST DABBING AND ROLLING BRUSHES

While we were adding the finishing touches to our first landscapes I thought of an interesting idea. On a small piece of cartridge paper or white cardboard about 15cm by 10cm some children were encouraged to build up a simple landscape by only rolling and dabbing bristle brushes. There were no limits on the size or kind of bristle brushes to be used.

"You don't need to draw or add any washed backgrounds. I just want you to add paint covered bristle brushes by dabbing and rolling them across the small sheet of paper. Let's just see what happens," said the teacher.

"Do you know what they will look like MrE?" asked Trent.

"No, I don't. I've never tried it before. I think I will have a go myself," he replied.

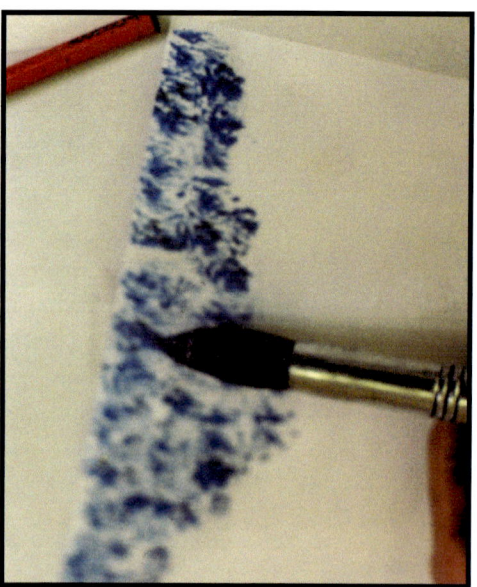

At least half a dozen children were quick to take up the challenge. Some of them could not resist drawing a foreground tree over the background before they painted it in. Mr E did not mind as we were trying something new. We were explorers finding new pathways in what for us, were unchartered waters.

I had spotted a couple of children looking at some of the books about artists. They were fascinated by artists who painted their pictures by using only coloured dots. I told them that they were painted at a time when it was fashionable to experiment with new ways of painting.

"Some tried to paint with hundreds of dots, others used little dabs and short strokes with their brushes."

"Can we try out some new ideas MrE?" they asked.

OUR OWN IMPRESSIONS OF A LANDSCAPE

BY THE RISDON VALE IMPRESSIONISTS

Mitchell B 10

Trent B 11

Louanne G 11

Joanne F 11

Emma J 10

THE RISDON BROOK DAM

A STORY OF OUR LANDSCAPES DEPICTING SCENES
FROM OUR LOCAL ENVIRONMENT

The day had dawned for our explorative journey to the Risdon Brook Dam. The day before, there had been a hive of activity as we prepared ourselves for the big day. Unfortunately, we were awakened to the sound of steady rain from heavily laden skies. Our prospects looked bleak. The faces on so many children looked as bleak as the weather as they put away their backpacks in the cloakroom.

LOCATION 1

"We are not going, are we?" asked a dispirited Matt.

No one liked rainy days. We had to stay inside all day. There was only a trickle of enthusiasm as they went about their morning tasks of a literary and mathematical nature. The teacher was reminded of his early days at Risdon Vale when so many of the children demonstrated that they had no wish to be there.

Fortunately, the teacher had prepared himself for such a calamity as this. A couple of weekends earlier, MrE had taken his family for a walk around the Risdon Brook Dam and spotted some suitable locations for our first Landscapes. He photographed them and brought the developed prints to school on the very same day of the excursion. Before the children had arrived, he photocopied and enlarged several prints in readiness for 'Plan B'.

LOCATION 2

LOCATION 3

During the lunch break most of the children were in the assembly hall watching a movie. It was still raining. Some remaining children helped their teacher rearrange the furniture to enable artistic activity. The tables in the activity room were set up for painting.

"What are we going to do MrE?" he was asked.

"It's a surprise," he answered.

On their return to the classroom for the afternoon session he told the children, "As we are unable to go to the Risdon Brook Dam, I shall bring the place back to our classroom."

He then placed his photos of the Risdon Brook Dam and their enlarged copies on the table before him.

"Wow! We are still going to paint the place after all."

"Now, on a piece of blank pad paper I would like you to draw the basic outline of a scene of your choice. All of the photos and copies are of the Risdon Brook Dam."

They were then encouraged to look at a coloured photo or black and white copy, identify the major outlines and draw them onto the blank pad paper. It was suggested that they write pencil notes on the paper that might help them with colour choices as well as the general shape of trees such as 'Fir Trees'.

The children were then asked to quarter their sheets into four grids, so that they could easily transfer their outlines to a piece of A 3 cartridge paper that also had been gridded using faint pencil lines. There was no further need to add written notes onto the cartridge paper.

The children were really engaged with their chosen drawings. They were also supportive of one another as their drawings progressed. The smiles on their faces told us the story. The misery of the morning was behind them. Yet the rain continued to fall from darkened skies.

Nicole and Trent chose to use drawing boards.
An outline of Location 3 with added notes

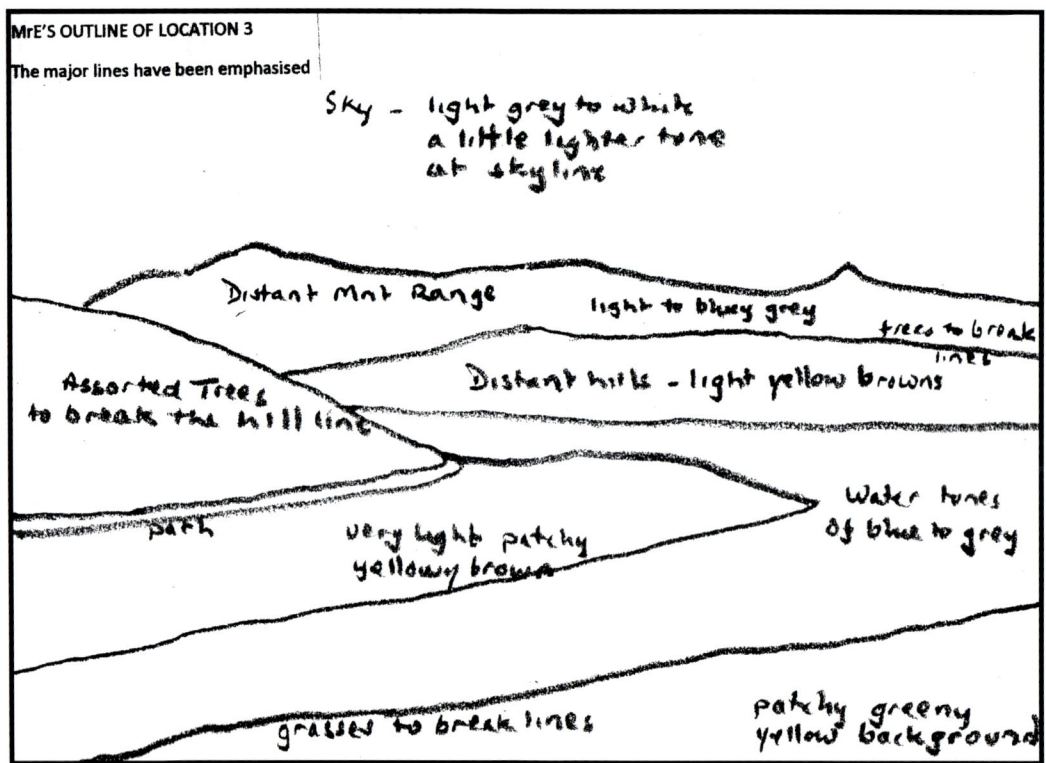

MrE's outline of Location 3
The lines have been darkened to facilitate a recognisable copy

Haylee, Blair, and Melissa preferred their sheets to lie flat on a table.
Some children tried two or three outlines of the available locations

It was now time to add powder paint to our transferred outlines on cartridge paper. With a relevant colour photo of the appropriate location and our noted outlines on pad paper as our guide, we followed a similar procedure as with our previous experience of washed backgrounds.

1. We gently washed the sky space with a mixture of blue to grey.
2. We added a foreground wash with a mix of yellowy, green, and brown.
3. We washed the surface of the water with a light bluey grey before we added the distant hills with a watery mix of yellowy browns. The far distant Mount Wellington would have appeared to be a light blue to grey.

Mitchell used broad brush strokes in sweeping left to right movements across the cartridge paper to lightly wash his space for water. His medium round bristle brush was a perfect choice to add a bluey grey with a hint of green to depict a rainy day.

The washed backgrounds were left to dry for a day or two. When we returned to our paintings Mr E demonstrated a subtle addition to the backgrounds. He used a moist middle sized bristle brush dipped in a mix of powder paint that was in harmony with the grassy area behind the dam.

"I am using short left to right brush strokes in patches across the sheet by the banks of the dam. I am using a mix of yellowy browns. This should enhance the appearance of the grass that has been effected by the lack of rain," said MrE with a smirk on his face.

The children laughed at the irony, as yet another rain shower passed us by outside.

I reckon the banks would look pretty green by now," added Josh.

The children were warned to avoid a complete covering of paint over their backgrounds.

"We must be sparing in our use of paint. We just want to enhance the backgrounds a little bit so that they are more interesting to look at," suggested MrE.

The children added similar touches to their previously washed backgrounds.

"If you look at the water you might see darker patches in places," added Mr E.

"Is that because the light is not getting in?" asked Danielle.

"Yes, it is," her teacher replied. "So, all you have to do is shade in a few darker patches to show a lack of light."

"What about reflections of trees in the water?" asked Brent. "They will look upside down, won't they?"

"You are right Brent," his teacher answered. "However, I think it would be better to add reflections a little later. Just add a darker patch in the water for the time being."

Danielle is adding detail to a foreground tree

Brent is finishing the painting of his fir trees. He is rolling a small bristle brush to create the effect of grasses below the trees.

ADDING FURTHER DETAILS

Our paintings were gradually built up over time. Each new session provided us with new possibilities for discovery and for the using of techniques that we had picked up along the way.

We were ready to paint the finishing touches to our paintings of the Risdon Brook Dam. We may well have begun by adding the appearance of distant trees. A little dab or two with a small round bristle brush lightly dipped a mix of blue and grey would do us fine. Middle distant trees would have required a slightly larger brush while the foreground fir trees would have grasped most of our attention. The fir trees were unlike any other trees that we had previously tried to paint. Some children sought the advice of Danielle and Brent who seemed to be relishing in their roles of supporting tutors. Some felt more at ease with the painting of gum trees instead. The notion of an artist's license was introduced. There was no necessity to paint a replica of the photographs even though they were an excellent supportive guide.

Some children added detail to the surface of the water. A large slightly moist bristle brush lightly in bluey grey would be dragged across the water space. Faint traces of speckled paint would remain thus giving an impression of variable light on the dam's surface.

TOGETHER WE LEARN

Mr E often liked to paint alongside the children. It helped him to feel part of the learning group as we were all learning together. Brent saw his teacher practicing the painting of some trees for the middle ground of his painting of the dam.

"I think you will be better off testing out a few fir trees," suggested Brent.

"You are quite right Brent. I haven't quite worked out how to paint fir trees," replied his teacher.

"Come with me MrE. I'll show you how," beckoned Brent.

The teacher followed and sat beside him at his workplace.

"You see MrE, they are a sort of triangle shape and some of the branches go sideways. They even bend down towards the ground in some places. You need only to paint in a few trunks and branches as you can't see the rest. For the leaves I just dab them on with a small bristle brush like what you told us before."

He was enthusiastic with his instructions and advice. He had worked that out for himself and was justly proud of his discoveries. His confidence and self-satisfaction glowed within his smiles as he continued with his painting. His teacher shared his pleasure.

The teacher had become the pupil. The pupil had become the teacher. Teachers and pupils teaching and learning together. That was the heartbeat of our learning environment. It was beating, beating, beating....................

"Thank you, Brent, you have been so helpful. I will take up your advice right away," said MrE as he returned to the testing of his fir trees.

When the paintings were finally finished, they were mounted and displayed on any available wall that we could find. Some of the paintings were framed in interchangeable frames made by a local frame maker and displayed in popular community locations.

"MrE, when will you take us out again so that we can sketch outlines for our next paintings?" asked Matt.

The winter months were closing in.

"I promise we shall have a whole day in Richmond next Spring," he replied. "The weather will be better then."

Two years later MrE took another group of children to the Risdon Brook Dam. We enjoyed lovely sunshine as we sketched our outlines for a new set of landscape paintings. The children seemed preoccupied with their eyes peering through viewfinders to help them identify and pencil in the major outlines. And so, the story begins again.

A WALK IN THE GALLERY

Mitchell had extended the height of two small foreground trees. His painting was improved by allowing his trees to break the skyline of the distant hills. In a sense his painting became his own rather than a confused replica of a photograph.

Mitchell B 12

Malinda B 11

Samantha T 10

Cade M 12

Danielle C 11

Blair G 11

Trent B 11

Adrian D 12

Matt B 11

Julian S 11

Brent S 10

Haylee O 11

MIXING COLOURS 4

ANOTHER LOOK AT COLOUR LINES

A couple of years back I tried a rather elaborate look at Colour Lines which showed a gradual progression of colour mixes from three related colours on the colour wheel.

First, we made up three colour lines that progressed from a Primary Colour to its neighbouring Secondary Colour and through to its neighbouring Primary colour.

PRIMARY .... SECONDARY .... PRIMARY

In this example, the centre square of the colour line was painted with the Secondary Colour 'PURPLE'. The Purple was mixed with equal proportions of Red and Blue. A pure 'RED' was painted on the extreme left of the Colour Line. A spot of true 'BLUE' was painted on the extreme right sided square. From the Red spot on the left, we gradually mixed and painted colour tones that slowly merged towards the Purple in the middle square. From the Purple centre spot, we painted spots of colour mixes that slowly merged into the blue tones before reaching the clearly defined Blue on the right extremity of the Colour Line. As this activity was a little time consuming, the children were encouraged to work in pairs or even in groups of three. This proved to be a testing time for collaborative learners.

Similarly, other Colour Lines were painted from PRIMARY 'YELLOW' to the SECONDARY 'ORANGE' and through to the PRIMARY 'RED'.

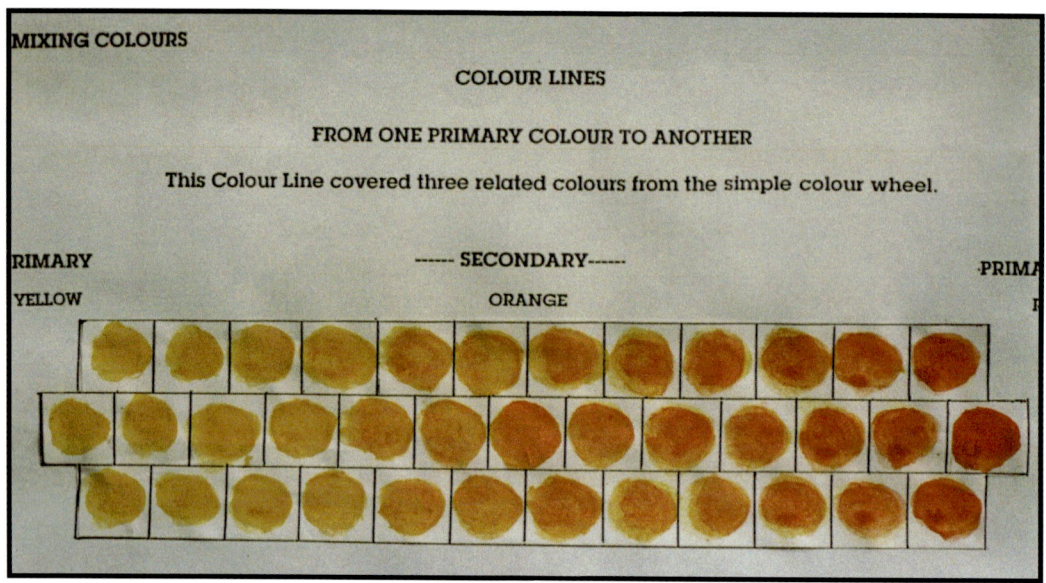

PRIMARY 'BLUE' ... SECONDARY 'GREEN' ... PRIMARY 'YELLOW'

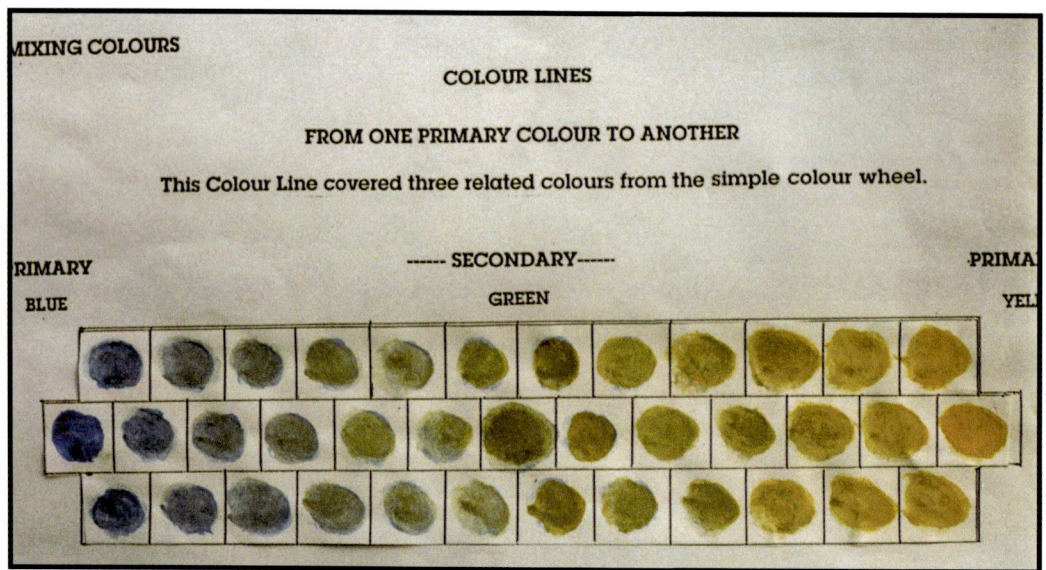

FROM ONE SECONDARY TO ANOTHER

This was followed by moving from SECONDARY to PRIMARY to SECONDARY

'GREEN' to 'BLUE' to 'PURPLE'

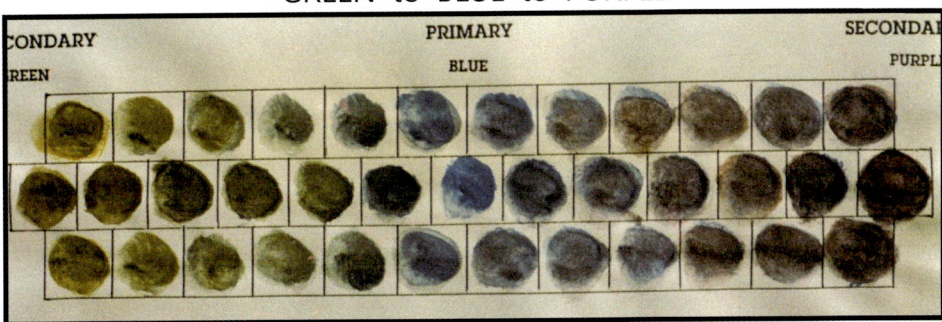

and 'ORANGE' to 'YELLOW' to 'GREEN'.

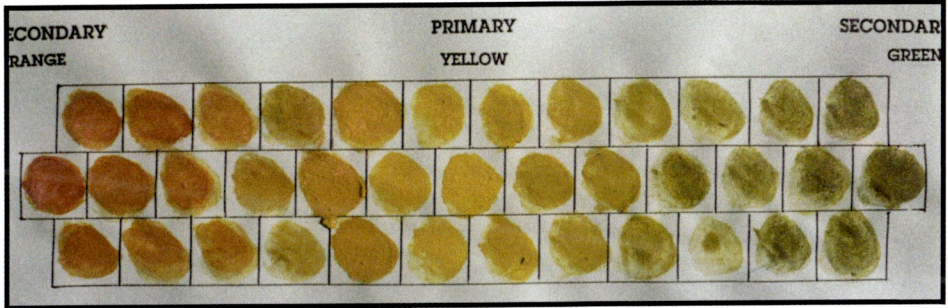

and 'PURPLE' to 'RED' to 'ORANGE',

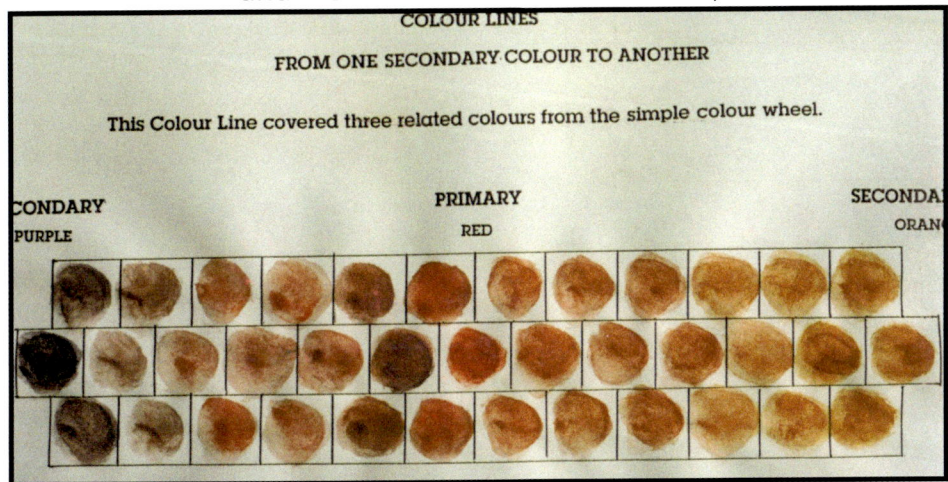

These paint mixing explorations provided wonderful opportunities for the discovery of colour tones and for learning the art of mixing them. The children were amazed to find so many tones of each colour. Many of these tones were mixed by varying the proportions of coloured powder paint. Some children may also have added a speck or two of black or white.

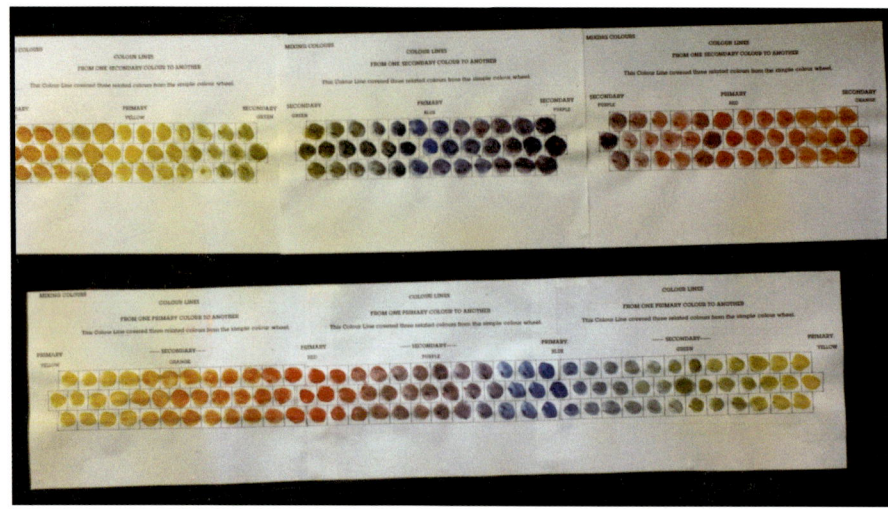

Then came the questions

"What would happen if we mixed all these colours together?" suggested Jamie.

"Surely, that would take an awful lot of mixing. How could you do it?" asked MrE.

"I know, we could join up a set of three colour lines and spin them around," added Julian.

"If we could find a way, what colour do you think the mixture would be?" asked their teacher.

"I reckon it will be a kind of muddy brown," suggested Melissa.

Three colour lines were joined together to form a cylindrical wheel.

"I wonder how we could spin the cylinder fast enough to make your muddy brown?" asked a rather doubtful teacher.

"We have an old record player at home," suggested Luke. "I'll bring it to school tomorrow."

"Yes! let's try that."

The children fixed a circular cardboard base to the cylindrical wheel. On the following day it was placed on an old turntable. The speed was set for 78 revs per minute and Luke turned it on.

We were so disappointed to find that the turntable was too slow for the colours to merge into a Muddy Brown. A photographed snapped at 1/125 th of a second only suggested that the photo was out of focus. We could still identify the merging colours. What on earth could we do?

"I wonder if we could use an electric drill. That will go faster," suggested Cade.

"I reckon an angle grinder will make it go even faster. My Dad's got one," added Justin.

"Shall I go and find Mr. Harrison? He will help us?" suggested Charles.

The questions and answers continued to flow, each revealing a growing understanding of not only our predicament but also the wonderful world of colours that surrounded us.

The school maintenance man soon arrived armed with an electric drill and an angle grinder. The cylindrical colour wheel was secured over a cardboard plate that was attached to the angle grinder. We all gathered around and waited in anticipation. The tension was mounting. He switched it on. In a flurry of immediate activity, the colour wheel spun off in shreds. The children gasped; the teacher sighed. That was the end of MrE's cylindrical colour wheel.

 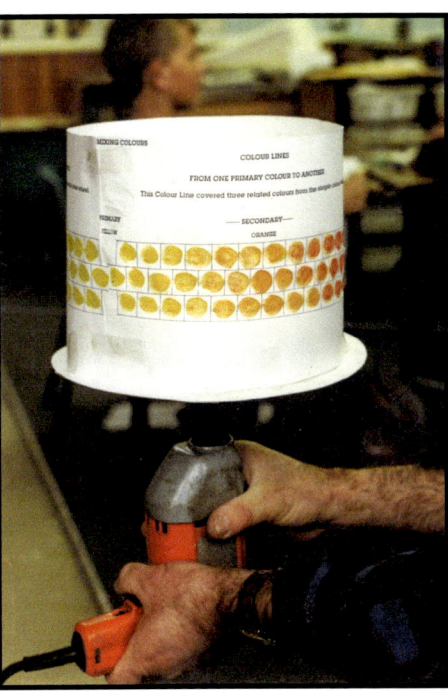

"It must have been too powerful. Let's use the drill?" suggested Julian.

"As long as it is ok for us to use your colour lines Julian."

So, it was agreed. Julian secured his cylindrical colour wheel to the cardboard plate that was attached to the drill. What was going to happen. The tension was high as eager faces awaited the impending disaster. It was turned on.

The drill proved to be more effective than the angle grinder. The spinning colour lines revealed a blurred, muddy yellow, or perhaps an optimistic tone of light brown. It was an anticlimax. The crowds gradually dispersed.

"Well, it's a kind of muddy brown"

The persistent group would not yet give up.

The children thought that they had found the elusive colour Brown. The discovery was theirs and without their input we might never have found it.

"I wonder how we could mix up a Brown by using powder paint," suggested Josh

"That is a great idea Josh," responded his teacher. "Let's try mixing the three Primary colours first and then we will add the Secondary colours later."

MrE suggested to a group of children that the Colour Wheel could be even further expanded.

"You mean that we mix two colours next to each other on the rim?" asked Josh seeking further clarification.

"We could mix three of them that are next to each other," put in Julian.

"It would be like throwing a stone into the Risdon Dam and watching the ripples spread out forming bigger circles," added Emma.

"Yes! that's right. So nicely put Emma," her teacher replied.

"I don't think we will have enough room to fit in another rim," said Ben.

STILL LOOKING FOR THAT 'MUDDY BROWN'

"I wonder if we could mix together all the colours that we have found so far," suggested Julian with growing impatience.

"I reckon it will turn out to be a lovely 'Muddy Brown' added Josh.

"I know what we should do next. Let's spin our expanded colour wheels. I'll find Mr Harrison and ask him to bring along his electric drill," suggested Brent.

On the obliging handyman's return, the gathering crowd encircled the man with the drill. An expanded Colour Wheel was correctly put in place. The revs worked up to maximum speed.

"There it is! Now that is a Muddy Brown. We have found it." High fives were shared by all.

The teacher still thought that their ecstatic cries of pleasure were a little optimistic. The children believed that they had found the elusive colour Brown and that was all that really mattered.

"I wonder how we could mix up a Brown using Powder paint?" asked MrE.

MIXING THE THREE PRIMARY COLOURS

"I wonder what colour we shall find by mixing the three Primary Colours"? asked the teacher.

"I reckon it will be that muddy brown again," said Brent

First, we tried to mix Blue, Red and Yellow in equal proportions. We found that this mix provided us with a lovely standard mix of 'Brown'. The teacher had prepared a worksheet so that they could keep a record of their findings.

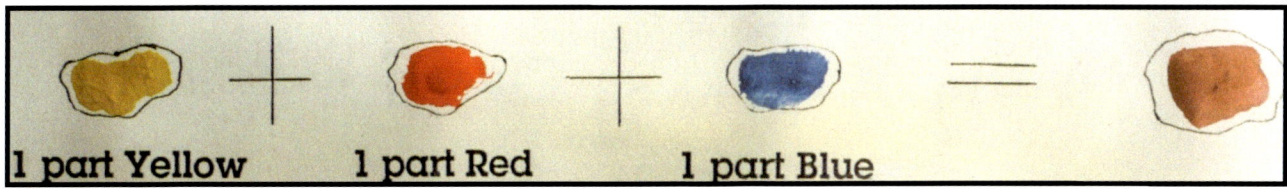

1 part Yellow   1 part Red   1 part Blue

We then experimented by controlling the proportions of each Primary colour to be mixed to form varying tones of 'Brown'. We found that more of 'Yellow' produced a lighter 'Brown', and more of 'Blue' gave us a darker tone of 'Brown'.

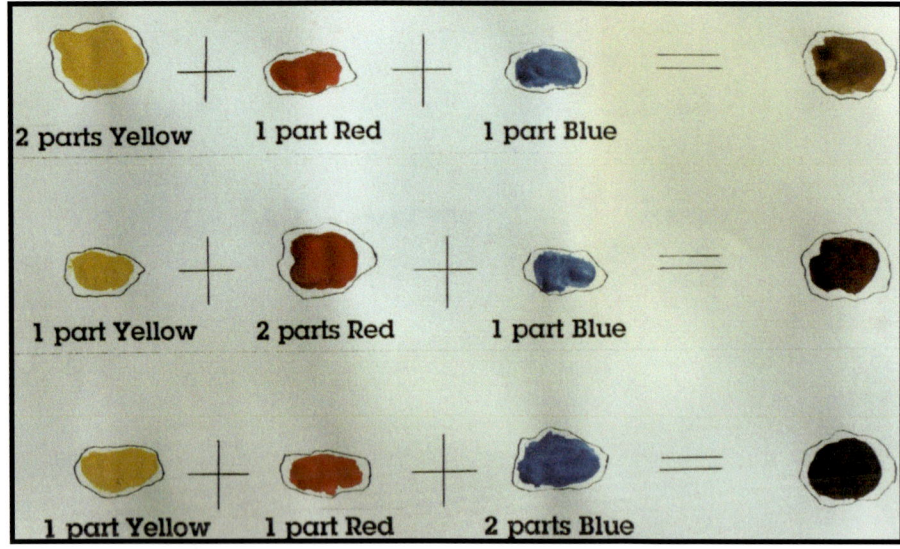 

The children were then challenged to discover further combinations of Red, Yellow and Blue. They were encouraged to predict the outcomes of their mixing of variable portions of Primary Colours.

Their teacher then informed them that the resulting mixture of three Primary Colours, "BROWN" was called a TERTIARY COLOUR.

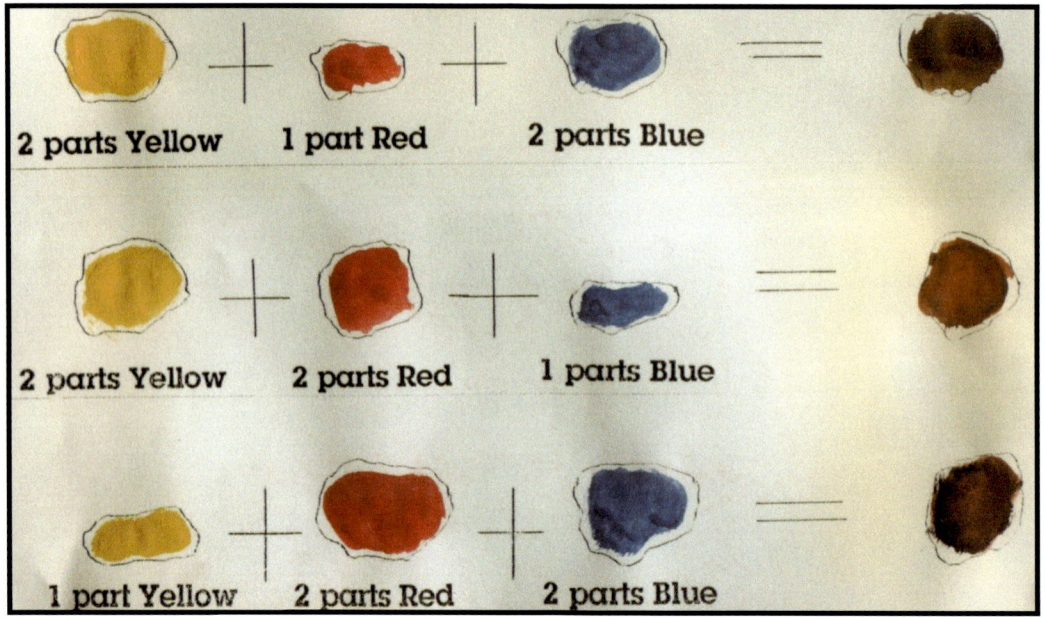

"It's like our educational institutions," he said. "The basic first stage of school is PRIMARY, like our Red, Yellow and Blue. The next stage of schooling is SECONDARY with our Oranges, Green and Purple. The third stage is for Higher Education, TERTIARY, like Universities or T.A.F.E. Colleges for our Browns."

"Were you a Brownie MrE?"

There followed a huge roar of laughter. It was such a clever play with words that their teacher laughed with them.

A MIXING OF SECONDARY COLOURS

"Let's now try mixing up Green, Orange and Purple," suggested Mr E. By mixing equal portions of the secondary colours we found this...

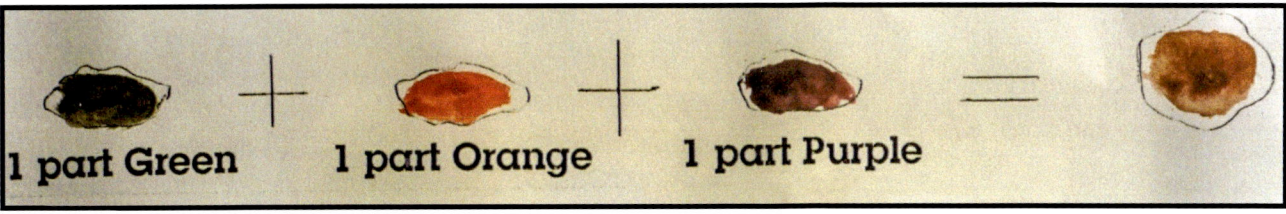

1 part Green   1 part Orange   1 part Purple

A lovely Muddy BROWN

For the benefit of artistic science, we shall call this a standard Brown.

We then tried mixing further combinations of secondary colours. We found even more tones of Brown. We found that two portions of Orange gave us a lighter shade of Brown and that two portions of Purple provided us with a darker tone of Brown.

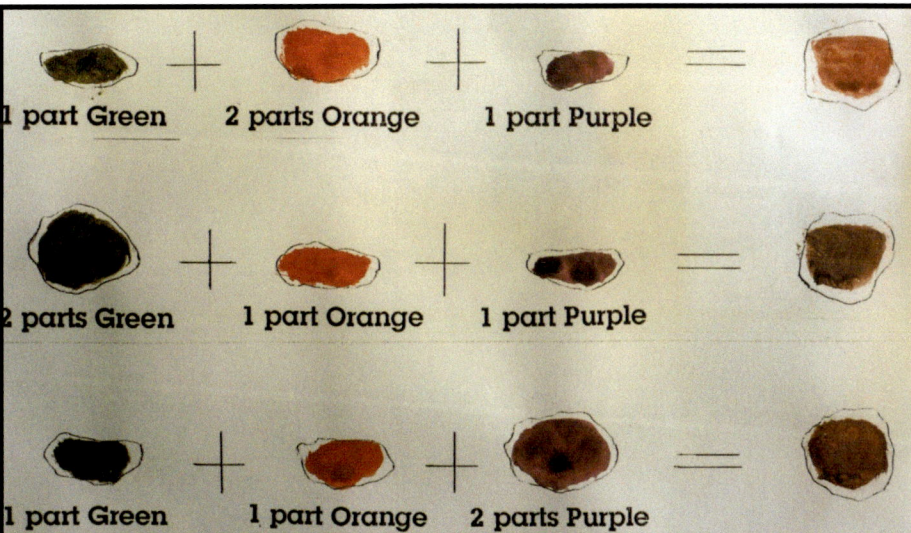

1 part Green   2 parts Orange   1 part Purple

2 parts Green   1 part Orange   1 part Purple

1 part Green   1 part Orange   2 parts Purple

The children added to their collection of paint mixing experiments by placing their work sheets in a mini folder that would eventually reside in their large Montage folders.

A MIX OF SIX

1 part YELLOW 1 part RED 1 part BLUE 1 part GREEN 1 part ORANGE 1 part PURPLE

"I wonder what colours we could try mixing next?"

"I know," shouted Julian who preferred to be called Jack. "We could mix the six colours from our first Colour Wheel."

He had been wanting to do this for ages. Jack was the first to mix all six colours; three Primary and three secondary colours in roughly equal portions. Other children quickly followed suit.

The teacher had spoken, "I wonder what colour will appear after all this mixing?"

"BROWN!! A MUDDY BROWN!!" they yelled.

"I knew already," said Jack, "I tried it out last week in secret and it worked."

"Now, I wonder what might happen if we mixed all the colours from the rim of the expanded Colour Wheel?"

"BROWN!!" they shouted.

"Don't you think we had better try it to make sure?"

"No, we already know," said Jack.

A host of Browns had been discovered. Some appropriately designed Colour Lines could be used to record some of our discovered tones of Brown.

Not long after that a small group came to me and asked whether they could paint a large Colour Lines of 'Browns'.

"I thought you might have had enough of mixing colours by now," suggested their teacher.

Their persistence was rewarded by Mr E promising to give them an appropriate recording sheet.

PAINTING TONES OF A TERTIARY COLOUR

BROWNS

This Brown in the centre was made by mixing 2 parts of Yellow with 1 part of Red and 1 part of Blue.

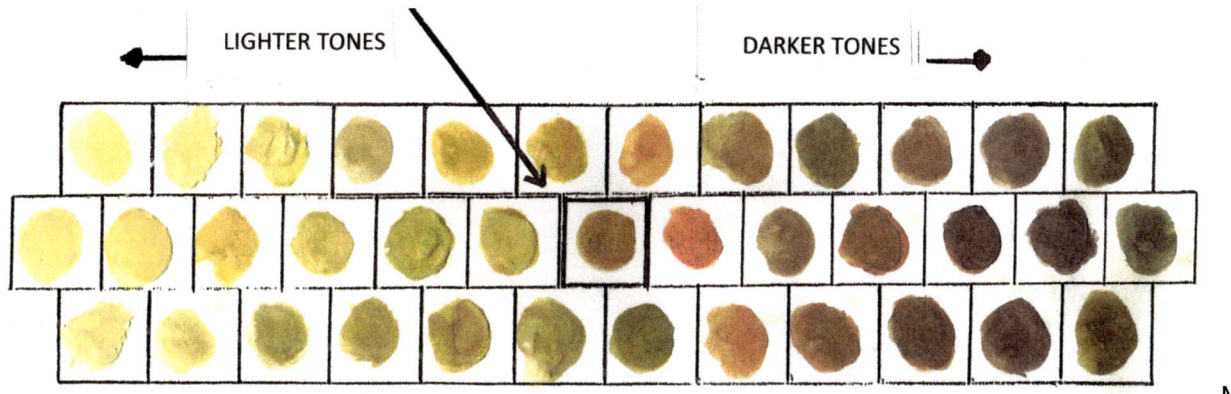

MrE

It may have been unreasonable to have expected an accurate grading of tones, but the small group of children was surprisingly good at it. They were encouraged to thicken their paint mixtures by reducing the amount of water in their brushes. And so, they created textures that were both pleasing to the eye and to the gentle touch of a finger.

REMEMBER

Practice on testing sheets before you apply a sample on to your colour line.

FROM PAINTING PICTURES WITH WORDS TO THE EXPRESSION OF THOUGHT AND FEELINGS WITH PAINT

IDIOMS

TOWARDS AN UNDERSTANDING OF IMAGERY

I first introduced an idiom "She's full of Beans." The children knew of course its meaning. However, what if the meaning was taken literally as might have been with a recently arrived visitor from Asia. The children laughed and were 'tickled pink' enough to collect their own idioms together with their own illustrations that humorously conveyed a literal meaning of the idiom. Much to their delight they soon discovered that the use of this simple form of imagery was both a conscious and subconscious part of thought and expression. Their conversations revealed a natural use of idioms that previously were often taken for granted. Their introduction to imagery was a fun time.

"LEFT HOLDING THE BAG"
MEANS: CAUGHT WITH THE EVIDENCE
Shane 11

"YOU'RE BARKING UP THE WRONG TREE"
MEANS: YOU HAVE THE WRONG IDEA
Malinda 11

"PULL YOUR SOCKS UP"
MEANS: TRY HARDER
David 11

"SWALLOW HOOK, LINE AND SINKER"
MEANS: SUCKED IN
Michael Age 11

"PUT YOUR THINKING CAP ON"
MEANS: TURN IT ON
Dwayne Age 10

"CAUGHT RED HANDED"
MEANS: CAUGHT WITH SOMETHING YOU
SHOULD NOT HAVE
Mitchell 10

"YOU ARE FLYING LOW"
MEANS: YOUR FLY IS UNDONE
Luke 10

The children were encouraged to illustrate their chosen idiom by drawing a literal interpretation. Underneath the drawing was placed the relevant meaning of the idiom

The use of coloured pencils and coloured marker pens proved to be popular choices. A few children chose to use pastels. They were encouraged to make their visual images large enough so they could be viewed from a reasonable distance. Sufficient space should have remained for the written idiom together with a simple explanation.

A GALLERY OF IDIOMS

Katie   +   Emma

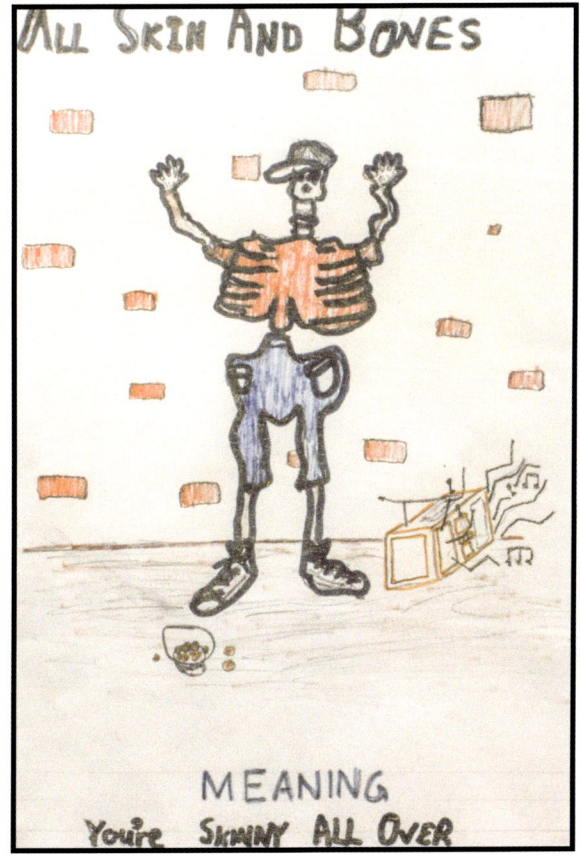

Kwenton

Lisa   +   Joanne

Brent S

Angela   +   Lauren

Luke C   +   Adrian D

Louanne G

Cassie D

USING IMAGERY TO EXPRESS THOUGHT AND FEELINGS

Idiomatic play was followed by exploring the idea of linking thoughts and feelings with images. Having listed some common thoughts and feelings the children put them in a context that allowed the image to sharpen the focus of the intended meaning.

LINE 1   SOMETIMES I FEEL   (The feeling linked to an image)
LINE 2   AS LONELY AS A STREET   (Elaborating upon the image to heighten meaning)
LINE 3   FULL OF 'FOR SALE' SIGNS   (no more than 6 words)

MrE

Sometimes I feel
as kind as a boy
letting me play with him.

David Blake 10

Sometimes I feel as
happy as a rabbit
in a field full of carrots.

Jessica Age 10

Sometimes I feel as sad
as a little baby
crying without its bottle.

Andrew Age 10

Sometimes I feel
as embarrassed as a cat
being chased by a mouse.

Louanne Age 10

Sometimes I feel
as lazy as a pig
laying in a mud puddle all day.

Emma Age 19

Sometimes I feel
as frightened as a tyre
speeding down a drag strip.

Ty Age 11

Sometimes I feel
as mad as a cat
who can't catch a mouse.

Joanne Age 11

Sometimes I feel
as free as a car
cruising at 120 k/h.

Jared Age 10

"SOMETIMES I FEEL......"

The children proceeded to develop a visual context for the presentation of their verbal play with thought, feeling and image. They were encouraged to draw the major features of their illustrations so that they loomed large enough to dominate the picture. The use of pastels again proved popular on A4 sized cartridge paper. After their three lined poems were proofread, the children printed them out and glued them over their drawings.

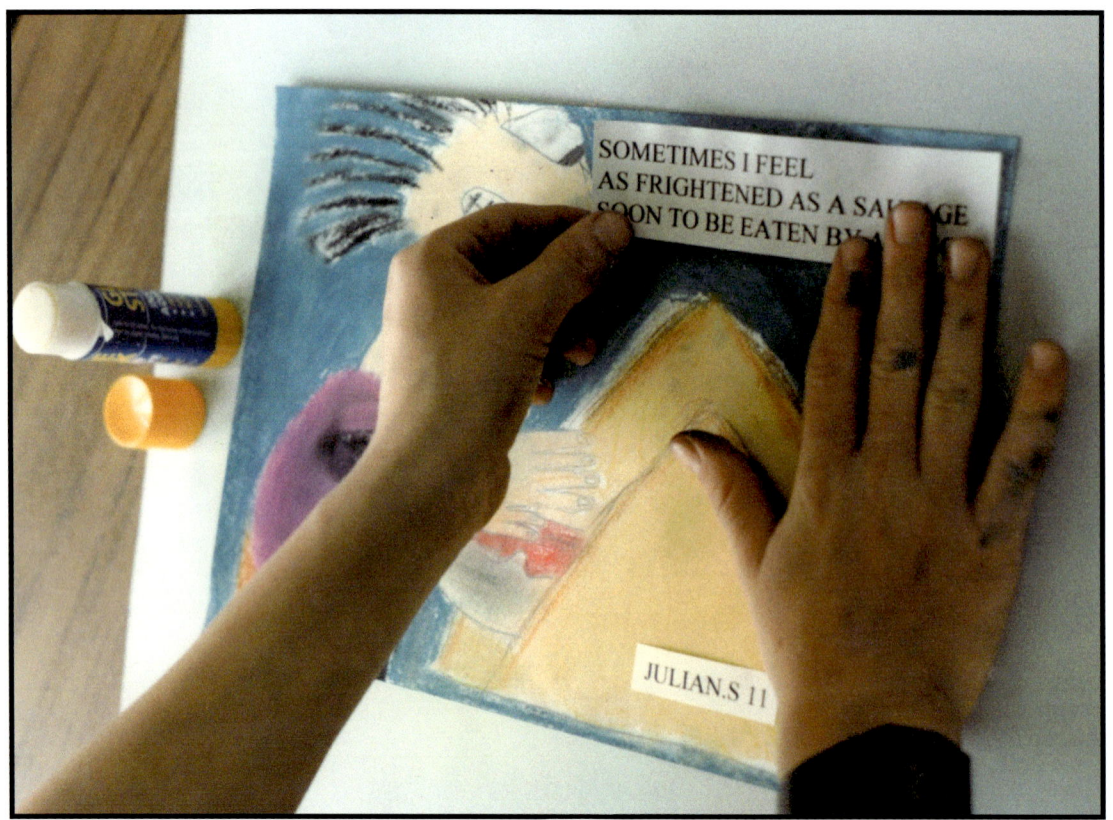

A GALLERY OF FEELINGS

Cassie D

Jackson O

Ty P

Julian S]

Jessica W

Ty P

Cade M

David B

Luke F

Julian S

Brent S

Sarah L

Danielle C

Luke F

Kwenton

Adrian D

Mitchell B

Jason

USING COLOUR, SHAPE AND LINE TO CONVEY FEELINGS

Our endeavours naturally flowed towards the expression of feelings by simply using colour, shape and line. The pictures alone had to convey the intended feelings.

A healthy discussion took place that linked colour with feelings. The following links were soon established.

SADNESS... Blue, Grey, and Black LONELINESS...... Blue, Purple, Green, and Grey

EXCITEMENT.....Red, Orange, Yellow, and Mauve ANGER.... Black, Red and Grey

LOVE... Pink, Red, Yellow and Blue

"What about 'FRUSTRATION'?" added Jack. "That's a good one isn't it"?

"Yes, it surely is Julian. Now what colours would you associate with 'Frustration'?"

"Oh, I think Red, Green and a bit of Black or Grey," he replied."

"What about 'FEAR'?" suggested Josh. "I am often scared at night."

"'ANGUISH' That's a good one," added Cade.

"What does that mean?" he was asked.

"It's like being tied up in knots," he replied. It's a sort of mixture of 'Rage' and 'Frustration'."

"Yes, you are right Cade. We often have mixed feelings, don't we?" MrE replied with a slight grin on his face.

"What about some nice feelings like 'Happiness'?" asked Danielle.

She was right. The children, particularly the boys, were keen to point out the darker feelings and they tended to avoid the softer ones.

"We should strike a balance between the darker and softer feelings if we can," said MrE in support of Danielle.

We then discussed the kind of shape and line that was appropriate for each feeling. Sharp jagged edges reflected 'Anger' and some of the darker feelings while softer shapes and wavy lines suggested the warmer feelings. The children were then invited to create their own pictures that expressed feelings without words.

Sarah's 'Anger' showed a subtle use of colour. A slight addition of purple to the red and black generated a greater interest together with some complexity of feeling.

Sarah L

Joel's expression of 'Gaiety' was enhanced by superimposing shaped outlines over his background.

Joel T

ANGER Danielle C 11

HAPPINESS
Sharyn G 10

Moving around the classroom and the adjoining activity room, I was made aware that we were still in need of a greater variety in the designing of our expression of feelings. We needed a more complex display of colour and shape. The children preferred to capture the most polarised of feelings. It was much easier for them to select the appropriate colour, shape and line for 'Anger' or 'Happiness' than it was for 'Disappointment' and 'Satisfaction'.

We talked about overlapping shapes and the consequent mixture of colours. We discussed appropriate colour choices for the less polarised of feelings. We talked of superimposing line and shape over a background. Soon their confidence and skills in expressing a variety of feelings spread in in ever widening circles like the rippling effect of a pebble cast into a pond. They enjoyed their drawings very much although some of the boys still leaned rather too closely to the darker side of human nature.

HAPPINESS
Christie H 11

CONFUSION Julian S 11

RAGE Danielle C 11

CONFUSION Cade M 11

JEALOUSY Danielle C 11

MISERY Joel T 11

LONELINESS Julian S 11

FROM PASTELS TO ACRYLIC PAINTS

Some of the children wished to express their feelings on a larger canvass using acrylic paint. They first painted a background and after it was dry, they added further details over the top of the background. They soon discovered that the painting of feelings was no longer the difficult barrier that at first confronted them. Like the intrepid explorers before them, they were pushing through the barriers to see what was on the other side; and the grass appeared to be greener.

The timely arrival of the use of acrylic paints enlivened their explorations into the world of feelings. The uninhibited discussions of their feelings surpassed their teacher's expectations.

"I have felt like that too when…" They freely talked about feelings as they were painting and relating them to their own experiences. They were equally interested in the feelings expressed by others. There gradually developed a mutual empathy and understanding of and for each other that surprised themselves and their teacher. Through the ensuing discussions they were able to further understand themselves, each other and the complex world that surrounded them

Justin is finger smudging a soft red pastel over a partial acrylic background.

The techniques that the children employed were also interesting. Many of them applied ideas that they had picked up earlier in the school year. Some covered their canvass with acrylic paint before superimposing further details. Some others explored the possibility of scratching out part of their design from recently applied acrylic paint.

Trent is brushing broad red strokes over his dried acrylic background.

A GALLERY OF FEELINGS

ENVY Trent 11

We thought that Trent had finished his painting of 'ENVY' but he continued by pushing a house paint brush laden with water on to the top of his painting, so that the water ran down the left side of his painting. He thought that the breaking of lines would create the 'WOW!' effect.

FEAR Chris S 11

Chris used a technique popular with younger children that helped them with the idea of "Symmetry". He painted one half of his picture and folded it over the back half the blank half of his sheet so that it covered the wet acrylic paint. It was then opened up to reveal his symmetrical painting. To paint half of a frontal view of a rat was an amazing feat for an eleven-year-old.

"We are all frightened of rats," he said. "So, I called it FEAR."

ANGER Shane A 11

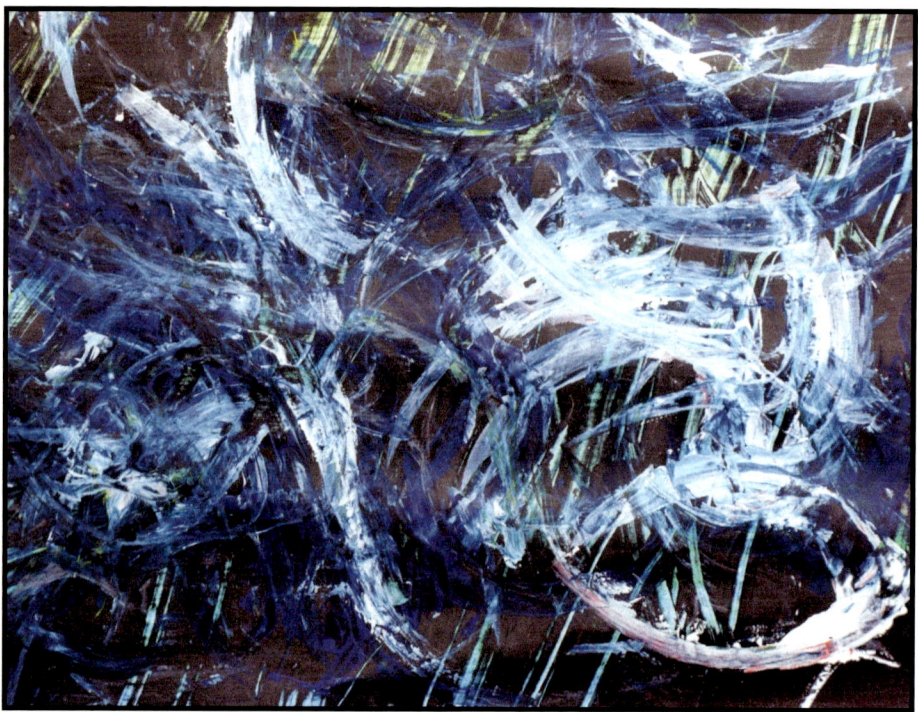

LONELINESS Justin M 12

Luke and Justin and Nick scratched out their details with a cardboard comb.

ANGER Nick 11

ANGER Matt B 11

AGGRESSION Luke S 11

LONELINESS Julian S 11

JOY Matt B 11

AGGRESSION Justin M 12

JOY Haylee O 11

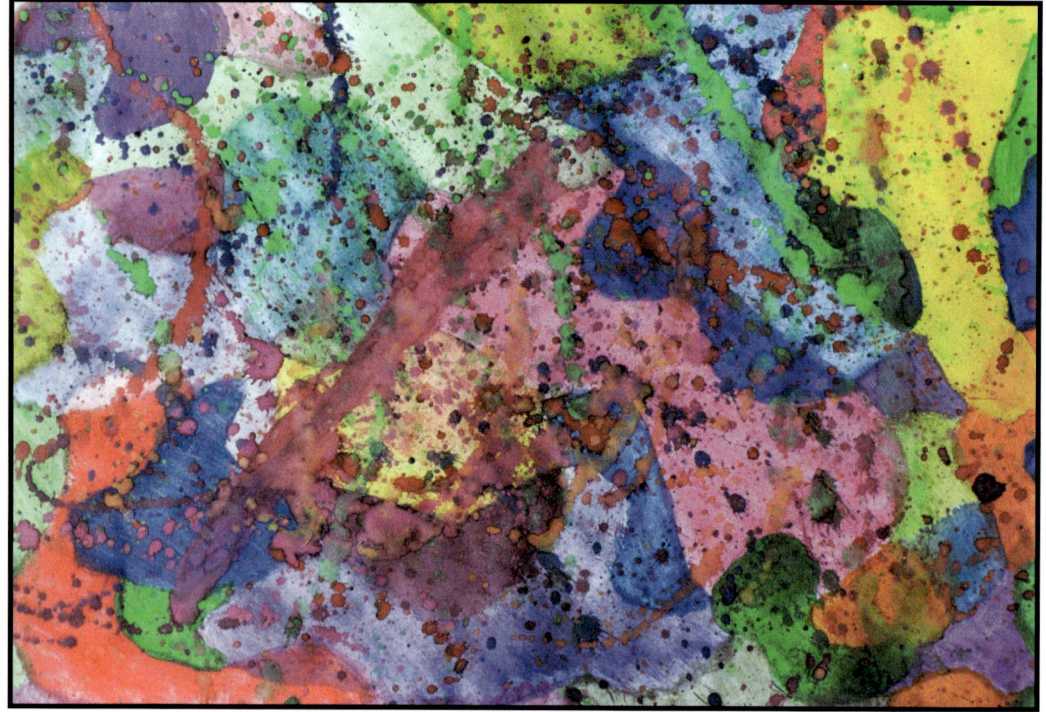

EXCITEMENT Blair C 11

JEALOUSY Sharyn G 11

CONFUSION Danielle C 11

PAINTINGS THAT REFLECT ISSUES OF CONCERN FOR YOUNG PEOPLE

"What are the matters that concern young people today?"

In small groups, the children discussed these issues before listing some of their concerns on paper.

During the 1980's I taught at the Taroona Primary school. It was and still, is a fashionable suburb of Hobart. It mainly housed professional people and business leaders. Unlike Risdon Vale, Taroona was a high socio-economic area. Naturally enough, matters of concern in part reflected the views of their parents and no doubt were frequently discussed around the dinner table at home. The matters of concern discussed in subsequent classroom meetings were mainly of a global nature. The children of Taroona were mainly concerned with environmental issues that threatened the future of our planet. Frequently mentioned issues were "World Peace", "River and Sea Pollution", "C.F.C.'s and the Ozone Hole", "Conservation of Forests", "Land Use" and "Pollution." Only a few children mentioned "Global Famine", "Cultural Rights for Aborigines" and "Drug Use."

The children were asked to choose a particular issue that concerned them and to express that concern with a sketch or two on a piece of pad paper. They were encouraged to express their thoughts and feelings without the use of words. The design had to be simple, dominant in size and subtle enough for admirers to discover the meaning for themselves. Gradually, the children developed an individual preference for a design that carried a strong and emotional impact. On an A3 sheet of cartridge paper, the children painted a background with a large house paint brush. Acrylic colours appropriate for their chosen concern were brushed in left to right movements across the sheet to maintain an even grain. If they chose more than one colour, the colours should have gradually merged into one another. On a subsequent day, their design was lightly sketched over the background and painted in using small bristle brushes. Smaller details were later superimposed over the design with smaller brushes.

The paintings slowly emerged over the period of a few days. Some children brushed varnish over their paintings to accentuate colour and image. The paintings were then double mounted and displayed. Their clever use of visual imagery highlighted their sincere concerns. Their teacher was deeply touched. The future of the world seemed safe in their hands.

TAROONA'S GALLERY OF CONCERNS

Joanne 11

Mathew 11

Jonathan 11

Georgina 10

Annabel 10

Michael 11

Alex 11

Anon

THE CONCERNS OF CHILDREN FROM RISDON VALE

Ten years later, and after the recent success with using images to reflect thought and feeling, I asked the children in my class at Risdon Vale to convey their thoughts and feelings about the world they lived in. In small groups, they first discussed and listed their matters of concern. On the presentation of their ideas their teacher was astonished by the uninhibited nature of their responses. They openly shared some of the darkest of concerns. They were both honest and sincere and perhaps their teacher should have better prepared himself for such a response. As he listened to their concerns, he soon realised that he and the school had to provide a positive response.

The teacher understood that Risdon Vale back in the 1990's was a third generation, housing commission community. Unemployment and incidents of social upheaval were high. The Neighbourhood Centre offered several social services and provided programmes to aid personal growth and promote self-esteem but the school itself could play a greater role in supporting children from such a needy community.

The children of Risdon Vale voiced a healthy concern for their immediate environment and the plight of injured animals by the roadside. However, no - one spoke of 'Word Peace' or showed any concern for hunger in third world countries. The children spoke of concerns that effected their own lives, their families, and friends as they saw it. Risdon Vale was their world, and their world was the source of their primary concerns.

More than half of our class agreed that their major concerns were "Drug Abuse," "Homeless Street Kids" and "Youth Suicide." The appointed group leaders would write down the salient features of their concerns. Their expressions may not have been articulate, but their meanings were sincere and clear.

POLLUTION

"We think that there is too much pollution in the world. Lots of sea animals are dying because people are polluting the water. Cars are also causing pollution because of all the smoke that comes out of them. I think we should have electric cars...."

"We don't like all the rubbish that is dumped in the bush at the back of Risdon Vale. Old and smashed up cars are left up there and there is lots of house rubbish up there."

DRUGS

"They are more deadly than cigarettes and are killing more people every year. Drugs that are mostly used around here are Heroin, Cocaine, Morowana and Speed."

"People try to sell drugs to me or my family and try to make out that they are somethink like tomato plants. Drugs make you do things that you haven't done before like go crazy and do things against the law. They give you health problems."

"Most people who take drugs get addicted to them and you can't live without them. Drugs are now affordable, now kids can buy drugs."

"The big kids from High School take drugs in our playground at night. We know, because they leave their syringes and stuff behind for someone else to pick up in the morning."

SUICIDE

"Some people do suicide because nobody likes them."

"Parents whose kids have committed suicide are blaming it on posters of Kurt Covain and because of what it says on the posters."

"A worry for me is that when something goes really wrong you might wish you were not here and wish you were dead. Some end up killing themselves. It's very foolish but it does happen."

STREET KIDS

"Parents usually make them leave home. When you look at a street kid you can see the sadness in their eyes. If you have never seen one, how would you know how they feel without a home or money and having to scab out of bins."

"I know kids who go up the bush at night and never come home."

The children obviously needed some support in the understanding and handling of their concerns. The teacher needed help and support with the provision of supportive learning experiences that would meet the children's needs and concerns. After discussions with the Principal, a Social Worker, and a support teacher from the regional office of The Department of Education, a suitable programme was devised. We were first to look at legal, illegal, and prescriptive drugs- their use and abuse. The matters relating to a boost in self-esteem were to receive a continued emphasis, building upon our successes with creative explorations in the Arts and Mathematics. We also needed to look at Peer Group Pressures, media influences and Responsible Decision Making. Parents of the children were notified, and they were supportive of our intentions. It was not long before we had a succession of visitors to our classroom. Each one was a specialist or expert in their own field. The children loved the idea that 'experts' and 'specialists' would take time to visit them and talk with them about their concerns. The children fully participated in the discussions and there was a continual flow of questions and answers. The teacher now felt more at ease with the situation now that he was receiving considerable support. It was about this time that the school and the Neighbourhood Centre combined to introduce a Breakfast Club. Some needy children were invited to join the club to ensure that they had a reasonable breakfast in the school assembly hall before school began.

One of our visitors in the late 1990's was a representative from the Drug Education Network. Elizabeth pointed out some disturbing details about drugs which under some restricted conditions were still considered to be legal. She pointed out some simple statistics concerning drug related deaths.

Of Drug related deaths for all ages in 1990's Australia

70% were related to Nicotine
26% were related to Alcohol
3% were related to Opiates
1% was 'Others'

Thus 90% of drug related deaths were from Nicotine and Alcohol. That fact alone stunned the children as the frequent use of both drugs permeated the atmosphere of most of their homes.

We then looked at drug related deaths for the ages of 15 - 34 yrs.

This revealed that 66% were related to Alcohol
23% were related to Opiates
11% were related to 'Others'

It was noted and understood that the effects of cigarette smoking would have taken some considerable time to influence a terminal illness. Heavy drinking over a long period of time would have been responsible for many deaths but the alarming death rate of 66% for 15 to 34 yr. old's, suggested that many of those deaths might have been caused by accidents induced by alcohol.

23% of drug related deaths from the use of opiates suggested we should have a genuine concern for our youth and young adults suffering from the use of such drugs.

Our guest teacher continued by explaining the term 'Standard Drinks' and further advised us on the safe drinking of Alcohol. Elizabeth also discussed with us the use of illegal drugs and the dangerous use of needles. Several pamphlets were left to re-enforce the obvious awareness that she had so much helped to develop.

I doubt very much that these statistics have improved very much in the last twenty-five years apart from a slight decline in cigarette smoking. I suspect that the present-day figures would be equally disturbing.

Hopefully, the growing foundations of their understanding about 'Drugs' would help to ensure the likelihood of informed, safe and responsible choices for their possible future use of drugs.

A survey on the children's' then current use of tobacco was less revealing. Cigarette smoking had become less socially acceptable in the mid 1990's. The advertising for cigarettes was by then restricted and was not so freely influential. However, peer pressure to entice experimental drug use was high. So, it was with cigarette smoking. At least one third of year 5 and 6 children at Risdon Vale freely admitted to the frequent smoking of cigarettes. At the conclusion of one of the meetings with the children in the 'reading corner' Mr E announced.

"From this very day, I shall stop smoking cigarettes."

He could no longer tolerate his own hypocrisy. He hasn't had a smoke since.

Adam was left pondering the number of standard drinks obtainable from a full bottle of wine.

Most of the class freely admitted that they had drunk alcohol. More than half indicated that they had drunk alcohol more than once a month. A quarter suggested that they had drunk it on a weekly basis.

"Are any of you aware of any advertisements for alcohol?" their teacher asked. He was met by an immediate class chorale imitating a well-known 'plug' for a Victorian Bitter. It had appeared that the children's concerns for drug abuse had led us to a timely intervention. Perhaps we had sown seeds for a future harvest of better health.

After our visitors had discussed some of their concerns, the children felt more at ease within themselves and for each other as if some dark clouds had passed us by without a drop of rain. The teacher considered the value of an artistic response to their concerns.

Any comparison between the artistic responses to the personal concerns of Taroona and Risdon Vale children would be an inappropriate exercise. The artistic responses were ten years apart and the nature of communities can change much within a decade. In 2000 it was well known that drug problems and low self - esteem permeate all communities – rich or poor. Affluence, or the lack of it, should be no yardstick for measuring the ills of our society.

Whenever we meet young children, we must in response be honest, compassionate, understanding, be willing to listen and offer useful support without being patronising or too judgmental. The role of the 'ARTS' today can and should be of significant value in support of the growing child. Indeed the 4th R might be the most undervalued 'ART' OR 'R' in education as we reach into the 21st Century.

"Would you like to do some acrylic paintings that might illustrate some of your concerns about the world you live in?" asked Mr E rather tentatively.

"Yes, Mr. E, I'll have a go," said Mitchell.

"I'll do one too. I'm going to do one about the Zinc Works on the other side of the river," added Josh.

"Do we have to do one about drugs or street kids?" asked Emma.

"You can choose any concern that makes you feel comfortable expressing," replied MrE.

The girls were joining in the discussion.

"Yes MrE, I'll have a try, but can I do mine with pastels?" asked Blair.

The children proceeded with the idea of expressing their matters of concern by sketching ideas on blank pad paper. It was hoped that the pictures themselves would illustrate the children's message making without the use of words.

Mitchell, Adrian, and Julian were off to a flying start. Within minutes they were transferring their pad paper design on to A3 Cartridge paper and painting in their backgrounds. The rest of the boys were trying out several designs on pad paper before their preference was transferred to an A4 Sheet of paper as a pastel drawing. The girls however were reluctant to move past the stage of drawing their initial designs. Most of them seemed unwilling participants. I think they have had enough of exploring the darker side of life. They longed for sunny days rather than the threat of dark clouds. I did not further push their involvement. They had travelled far enough.

Julian chose a rather large Weightlifter under the influence of steroids.

Damien chose a drug addict having a fix while Mitchell chose the plight of a street kid as his subject.

Mitchell chose an acrylic background of blue, red, and black.

Damien is adding details to his multicoloured background.

Julian is adding details to the face of his weightlifter.

Some of the boys displayed a subtlety of thought and feeling and were quite perceptive in their use of visual imagery. Adrian's "A fix with a syringe," showed the user's face reflected in the spoon. 'I wonder what it was going to say'?

Adrian D 11

Julian S 11

Mitchell B 11

'Street Kid', his cigarette smoke drifted upwards to the darkest of skies. The ground was sky blue. Thus, Mitchell was suggesting that his world was upside down.

These three boys were keen to do some more. Adrian tried one of a beer drinker, but he felt that he had to include a subtitle to add meaning to his painting. The boys really took a liking to the pastel drawings of people in a mess. They all felt that they needed an added caption to carry their meaning to the viewer. It then degenerated into who might out do the other with their outrageous personifications of alcohol abuse. Mitchell however, kept his own council and constructed an excellent picture of the zinc works. His foreground showing the zinc works was made from cut out black paper above which were dark pastel skies. Emma was the only girl to hand to me her picture of a girl smoking cigarettes. I felt that our day was done. It was time to move on.

A WALK IN THE GALLERY OF CONCERNS

Mitchell B 11

"Factories must try harder to control the smoke going up into our atmosphere."

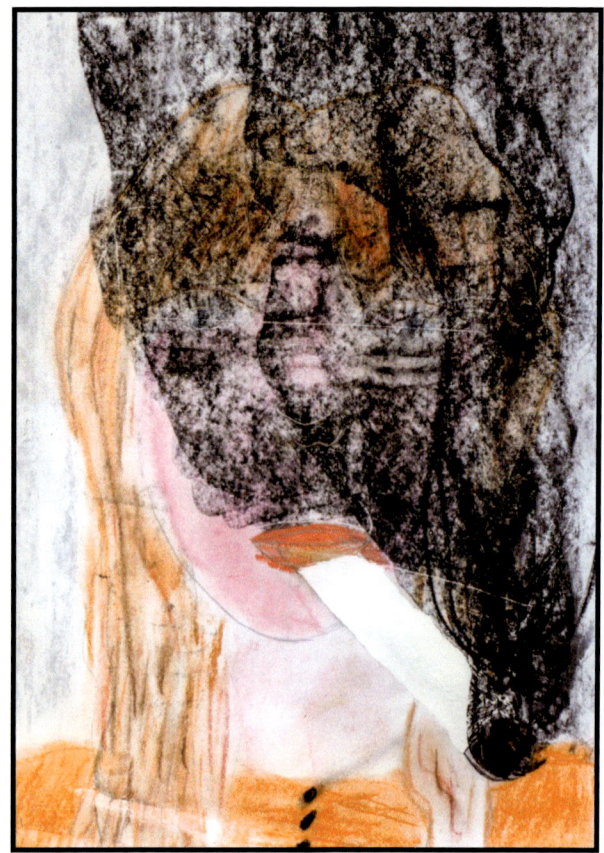

Emma J 11

"Smoke gets in your eyes and in your lungs."

Joshua P 11

"I you get too drunk in the tavern you will get kicked out."

Adrian D 11

"If you drink and drive you could put other people at risk."

Brent S 11

"If you smoke too much the tar will stick to your lungs and make breathing difficult."

Cade M 11

"We can't catch any fish when the rivers are so polluted."

Mitchell B 11

"Nicotine is addictive, but the tar is what kills you."

David B 11

It's sad to see so many car wrecks dumped in the bush around Risdon Vale

Julian S 11

"If you drink too much beer you will feel sick and vomit."

MrE stood by the window watching the rain fall from darkened skies.
"What's the matter MrE? You look sad," asked Emma. "Don't you wish it won't rain anymore?"
"Yes!" he said emphatically, "It's time we looked for sunny skies."
"I know what you mean MrE. Let's do something really nice next week."
"I think we might try some Still Life drawings next week," he replied.

FOR SOME, A MOMENT
OF LIGHT RELIEF

I remember the moment well. It was late August in Tasmania, and the wintry sunshine beckoned the impending arrival of Spring. We had recently completed our unit of work "Matters of Concerns". It was a Friday morning, and we were busily engaged in activities associated with "Maths Workshop". Some children were sitting on the classroom floor measuring the size of the furniture that covered the floor space. Their goal was to create a floor map of the classroom to a scale of 1cm – 50 cm. As their teacher bent down to see how they were going, there followed a ripping sound of a huge fart. He had split the seam of his pants.

"Oh MrEEEEEEEEE...!!!," was the cry that was soon followed by an explosion of uncontrolled laughter.

"That was a good one MrE."

He stood up and smiled, but before he had a chance of reply one of the boys shouted,

"Mr E! You have blown a huge hole in your pants. We can see the colour of your underpants."

There followed such raucous laughter that Mr E's cheeks had turned to pink. All he could do was laugh with them and share their moments of merriment. He then retrieved his jumper from the chair behind his desk and tied it around his waist to retain his modesty. He would have to wear his jumper like that for the rest of the day.

The bell rang and to his relief it was morning play time. The laughter followed the children out into the playground. No doubt their embellished stories would continue to ring around the playground. By the end of the day the whole school had heard about it. Thank goodness the week - end was nigh as MrE was sorely in need of some recovery time.

WHAT TO DO NEXT

There was about a month left of the winter term. We still had time to begin our first clay vases and bowls. Then they would have time to dry during the holidays before being fired in the high school kiln in the spring. There was also time to set up a display in the Activity room for 'Still Life' drawing so that three or four children could sit around it at a time.

By this time of the year our four- pronged series of creative explorations were having a profound effect on the children.

Prongs 1 ARTISTIC EXPLORATIONS
       2 MATHEMATICAL EXPLORATIONS
       3 PRACTICAL EXPLORATIONS (Making things with your hands e.g., Building Bridges out of paper and cardboard.)
       4 CREATIVE EXPLORATIONS FOR CHILDREN WRITING

The children were often very busy working at several stations set up around the two rooms. They liked the choice of activities; they equally enjoyed creative explorations on their own or by collaborating with one another. They were learning to belong to each other through our manner of co-operative learning. They believed that their lives mattered and realised that our progress was hastened by the mutual support given and received. They more readily accepted their differences and were more tolerant of each other. They were far more positive about their school life and their social skills grew in abundance. It was a natural consequence of our approach to learning.

RICHMOND

The winter months had passed us by, and spring had returned bringing warmer weather and sunshine. The teacher was about to deliver on his promise of a day trip to Richmond.

Our backpacks were filled with extra clothing, drink bottles, lunches, clipboards, pad paper and a variety of soft pencils. The teacher also took with him a couple of teacher aides and some chosen parents for support. Each supportive adult was provided with a copy of Granny Jones' booklet "GOSSIP AND FACTS ABOUT RICHMOND." This was an excellent little booklet of stories, historical photographs, maps, and notes about many of the buildings and people of Richmond Town.

Our bus dropped us off at the old Richmond Jail for a ten o'clock appointment with our guide. He told us that the jail was five years older than Port Arthur and it remained as a prison until 1928. A few of us were locked in a kind of barn surrounded by damp stone walls covered in scratch marks.

"This is where some of the prisoners slept at night," our guide said.

Then he turned his torch off and it was very dark.

"Many nasty things happened in here at night. Many say that this place is haunted," he continued.

The ensuing screams forced him to switch on his torch before letting us out into the bright sunlight.

"Now we can't see. It's so bright outside," said Cade.

After our chilly experience in the jail, we embarked on a historical trail around the back streets of Richmond. Using Granny's guide, we identified some of the old buildings and the stories behind them. By the time we had reached the banks of the Coal River it was lunch time.

After lunch, MrE had chosen a lovely view of the oldest bridge in Australia for our first lot of sketches. With a viewfinder in hand, he reminded the children of its purpose.

"The idea is that the view we see through the viewfinder corresponds with the sketch on our pad paper."

"Like we did at school sketching the trees in the playground," added Luke.

"Yes, that's right Luke."

Clues were also provided to help the children with their starting points by seeking out the major outlines such as, the bridge top, riverbanks, and the arches of the bridge. If they wished, they could add further details and some accentuated shading, e.g., under the arches of the bridge. Popular soft pencils proved to be 4B and 6B.

"Now, off you go and find your own little spot within twenty – five meters of here and draw your major outlines of the bridge as you see it. Please remember to add notes about shady areas and colour variations e.g., the river and the bridge. That would be a great help for when we try some painting back at school."

The teacher took off with his camera to photograph the children sketching the bridge before returning to lend further support and guidance.

We then sketched views from the other side of the bridge. Most of us had sketched two or three outlines with a few added details before it was time to move on. We had about an hour left before the bus was due to meet us at the car park.

The story of the bridge was told and then we split into small groups to walk down Bridge Street to identify the older looking buildings that had stories to tell. Most of the buildings had been used for many fascinating purposes before this present day's primary attention; "The seeking of the tourist's dollar." Granny Jones had served us well.

On the bus back to school we sang our made-up songs about old Richmond Town to popular tunes of modern times.

"Thank you everyone for helping us to make this day such a good one," said MrE. "See you all tomorrow."

"Thanks, MrE! It was real good," some shouted in unison.

BACK AT SCHOOL

On our return to the classroom, we first tidied up our sketches by adding further details such as some subtle shading of the bridge's arches and a few reflections found in the water. Photographs helped to keep our recent experiences alive and proved to be a most useful guide and reference.

The children gradually composed their drawings and/or paintings over a period of approximately three weeks. Having selected their view of the bridge for a painting they would have first transferred the drawn outlines onto a sheet of A 3 cartridge paper.

Those who wished to compose a drawing of the bridge in soft pencil or pastel simply added further details until they were happy with their finished product.

Those children who chose to paint their scene of the bridge, followed by adding light washes for the sky and foreground in a similar manner to their experience with the Risdon Brook dam. Then later, they would have painted in the required details using smaller soft haired or bristle brushes. Previous experience had served them well.

The children were well spread out in both the classroom and the activity room. They were often seen and heard to be offering support and advice to one another, but never did they touch with a brush, a painting that was not their own. The teacher was often on the move from table to table providing encouragement and advice until in need of a rest he would sit down and continue with his own painting of the Richmond bridge. Then the children would come to him and offer the same supportive encouragement.

Questions, answers, and praise were all part of the continual buzz of the classroom that was often quietly supported by the distant sounds of Bach or Vivaldi.

The teacher himself would often attempt drawings and paintings so that his suggested techniques could be modelled and easily followed by keenly observant children.

Over the three weeks of Richmond activities the children would have completed at least two drawings or paintings. Some of them chose to paint or draw some of the old buildings in Bridge Street using old or recent photographs as a guide. To complement these artistic responses the children were asked to complete a piece of research on one of the following topics.

"The Richmond Jail," "The oldest bridge in Australia,"

"The story of a Richmond building," or "Tourism in Richmond today."

IN A MESS AND OUT OF A MESS

However, during one afternoon of artistic exploration there was a little incident that momentarily stunned us all.

"Oh shit! I've fucked it up," came the anguished cry. "My painting's ruined."

There followed a stunned silence. All we could hear were the strains of a Bach's Brandenburg Concerto. MrE was sitting two tables away. Eyes were flickering back and forth from Kaycee to MrE. What was he going to do?

He quickly moved over to her table, sat beside her, and looked carefully at the colourful, watery blobs that stained her sky wash. It may have been caused by a slight distraction or a flying elbow as they were sitting rather close to each other.

"We can fix that Kaycee. Could someone please quickly pass me a large dry bristle brush, a soft haired brush and a container of clean water."

"I'm sorry MrE, I shouldn't have said that. It was a horrible surprise."

"OK Kaycee, it is your painting, and I will show you, how you can repair the damage. 'Let's keep our cool." He was handed the items he asked for and continued by saying

"Now Kaycee, I want you to take this dry bristle brush and very gently dab it over the watery mess."

"Like this MrE?"

He nodded his reply.

"Wow! it's soaking up the water," she observed.

"Now continue to dab it until you are left with just a dirty looking stain. That's good. Now, I want you to take hold of this soft haired brush, dip it in clean water and gently wash over the stain in gentle left to right movements."

"The stain is disappearing MrE. My painting has been saved. Thankyou MrE.
Oh, I'm sorry about the swearing."
Kaycee was so pleased as her painting had meant so much to her.
"I have said similar things on the golf course Kaycee, so I know what it is like to be really disappointed. But we must be careful to mind our choice of language in the classroom. Is that Ok with you?"

"Yes MrE, you are right," she said with a wink and a smile from ear to ear.

It was not long before Kaycee had cleaned up her misfortune. The watery dark blob seemed to have melted into her washed clean sky. The remaining stain matched her grey skies. She felt free and at ease to continue with her painting of the Richmond bridge.

On the following afternoon Mr E spilt some dirty coloured water over the sky wash of his painting to demonstrate the procedure to the rest of the class. Some of them had already a pretty good idea. He had also written a sheet of guidelines if any such incidents should arise again.

REMEMBER!

WHEN SOMETHING GOES WRONG, FOLLOW THIS ADVICE

1. Keep your cool. Try not to swear and avoid seeking blame or revenge.
2. Don't give up, rip it up and say, "It's ruined, I'm hopeless." More likely, something could be done to keep your good work alive.
3. If you can, fix it yourself straight away by using the methods that have previously been suggested by your teacher.
4. If you are uncertain as to what action to take, seek advice and support from someone who might know what to do. That might be a talented friend, a supporting adult, or your teacher.
5. Give other children praise, support, and encouragement for their efforts, so they in turn might do the same for you. It just makes everyone feel better.

These points of advice were copied and placed on strategic display in the classroom and adjoining activity room. I did not remember hearing any swearing in the classroom after that. In the playground it was rather a different matter. There, I would have turned a deaf ear to bad language unless it was directed at someone with an intent to hurt their feelings. For most of them, they were using the language of their community. If I had acted on a poor choice of language by disciplining the girl in the classroom, the problem with her painting might never have been solved. She was not swearing at anybody. It was an act of self - admonishment. The teacher was pleased that he had acted in such a manner. So, too was Kaycee and the rest of the class.

Within four weeks of our day trip to Richmond our paintings, drawings and research tasks had been completed. Their works, including the photographs, were mounted, and displayed so that they dominated the walls of the classroom and the activity room. It was a massive creative response to our visit to Richmond. It deserved the appreciation of many who took the time to visit us.

A WALK IN THE GALLERY

Ty P 12

Jason

Sound socially supportive skills need time and patience to develop. Quite a few children, particularly those from low socio- economic backgrounds have an impulsive streak in their nature. Their instinctive reactions might often include 'the eye in exchange for an eye.' Slowly but surely, the children were supported in the belief that considered alternative options of mutual support were more beneficial to themselves, to each other and for the whole developing learning environment that was substantially the pumping heart of our classroom's existence. Co-operation and collaboration maintained the gentle throbbing pulse that helped so much to bring about the necessary change in the children's attitude and behaviour. Our creative explorations in ART, MATHEMATICS and PRACTICAL CHALLENGES OF A SCIENTIFIC NATURE, all provided us with the stage upon which, we the players, learned our parts.

THE BRIDGE

PENCIL SKETCHES

Cassie D 12

PASTEL DRAWINGS

Dwayne F 11

Jason 10

Jared 10

PAINTINGS

Stefan T 12

Joanne F 11

David B 11

Lauren B 11

Louanne G 11

Cassie D 12

PENCIL SKETCHES

BRIDGE STREET

Ty P 12

DRAWINGS

Luke C 11

Jared 10

PAINTINGS

Jason 10

Ty P 12

A QUESTION OF OWNERSHIP

I often sat alongside the children and tried to paint the pictures that the children were painting. I was amongst them, and in tune with them as I tested my colour mixes on a piece of blank A4 pad paper. Some sat beside their teacher and watched and chatted to him as his landscape appeared to grow in shape, form and colour.

"MrE! can you help me. I'm not sure if my background hills look right."

"Yes, I'll come over right away."

He stood up and sat alongside Cade.

"I think your sky is looking just fine, but I think your distant hills are too bright in colour. I can see your choice of bluey grey with a dash of purple is excellent, but we need to tone it down a bit. Come over to the window and I'll show you what I mean," suggested his teacher.

Standing at the window he said, "Now look over to the far distant hills and you can see that they are very pale in colour."

"Yes, I can, that's because they are so very far away. Isn't that right MrE? They look like a pale bluey grey. But how can I make my painting look like that?"

Back at his table Mr E demonstrated his possible solution on a piece of testing paper. He painted some hills in a colour tone that was too rich.

"Now, watch this," said MrE as a few more children gathered around. With a large clean bristle brush dipped in clean water he proceeded to gently brush across the distant hills. The hills were becoming much softer in tone.

"Now Cade, you can try it on your own painting, but remember to be very gentle with your brush strokes."

He did just that with considerable success. He smiled and his teacher could feel his happiness. The point to be made is, that some teachers and parents would have demonstrated the idea directly onto the child's painting. Sadly, the ownership of the painting would have been taken from the child. It was no longer his painting. It would belong to the adult and the child. We all try very hard to respect the ownership of our paintings. We all have pleasure in supporting each other with a helping hand but our demonstrations are always on a piece of testing paper.

DISPLAYS

We celebrated the completion of our drawings and paintings by ensuring that due care and thought was given to their preparation for display in a variety of locations. Appreciative children were further inspired by the imaginative attention that their works deserved. An attractive display and its consequential recognition would have invited much needed boosts to their self-esteem and confidence. Such displays would have provided sufficient stimuli for others to be influenced by our artistic ideas and the manner of their presentation. Our displays grew from the classroom walls and often spread to the corridors and the school assembly hall. Some of our works have been regularly displayed in business and service centres throughout the local community. On a rare occasion our work has been displayed in an art gallery and on the walls of an office in Parliament House, Canberra.

The children in our classroom produced a considerable amount of work that deserved to be displayed. Classroom displays reflected nearly all the work across the curriculum. These would include their writing of experiences, Maths Workshop activities, Scientific explorations, Research and of course their artistic endeavours. A teacher and his teaching aide would have insufficient time to mount and display that amount of work. The children were shown how to mount their own work and after a little practice over a month or two they became very proficient at it.

A paper cutter was used to square off the edges of the painting. The work was then carefully stapled or glued onto white backing paper so that there was an even border of about two centimetres. The use of staples certainly saved time but they tended to disfigure the appearance of the mounted work. The use of staples also allowed the mounting papers to be recycled. Our general rule was if the works were to be framed for community display, then we would use glue instead of using staples. A moderate use of glue certainly enhanced the appearance of their paintings. The use of brightly coloured backing paper was discouraged as our attention would have been diverted away from the painting. We preferred the use of white or cream paper or cardboard for single mounts. A border line drawn with a metre ruler and black or grey marker pen about one centimetre away from the painting's edge often provided a most effective finishing touch.

MOUNTING PAINTINGS

SINGLE MOUNTS

Damien is supporting a younger boy as he adds a drawn borderline to a single mounted painting.

DOUBLE MOUNTS

In most cases our first mount was on cream or white paper leaving a border of two to four centimetres. The second mount was over grey or soft pastel coloured cover paper with a border of similar width. Occasionally, black cover paper was preferred but there was a danger that its appearance would be a little strident. If some of the paintings became a little warped as they dried, then the use of time saving staples proved to be a popular and acceptable choice. Quite often the children mounted their own work. Occasionally, they worked in small groups to recover a backlog of unmounted work.

A COLLABORATIVE ATTEMPT TO DOUBLE
MOUNT AN ACRYLIC PAINTING

It was a rewarding experience for the teacher to witness the children working in co-operative teams to prepare their works for display. This enabled the children to feel a greater sense of ownership and control over their creative experiences. If the children were too busy to mount their work, then we could call upon support from the teacher aides and some supportive parents.

An 'Assembly Line' at work. One in control of the paper cutter, a second fitting the first mount on to white paper and the third stapling the first mount on to grey backing paper to complete the second mount.

After Christie's painting had been completed, a team of two boys quickly brushed over the back of her painting with cardboard glue. Then they carefully turned over the painting and placed and pressed it over some suitable white backing cardboard. It was then trimmed with a paper cutter to give us a 3cm wide border.

Julian and Mitchell then offered their assistance. The back of the single mounted painting was glued again before being turned over, placed, and firmly pressed over the black cover paper.

The black cover paper was trimmed with a paper cutter to create an even border before the completed mount was presented to a proud owner. A smiling Christie was both appreciative and keen to show off her painting. Her self-esteem was high. The boys had presented her with an excellent demonstration. Christie could in the future be responsible for mounting her own work knowing that support if required would have been readily accessible.

Children loved painting with thick, creamy, and brightly coloured acrylic paints. If they painted over litho paper or even quality cartridge paper, it often resulted in the paper becoming warped or torn and therefore difficult to mount. The purchase of suitable cardboard proved to be expensive. So, resourceful teachers had to be good scroungers.

A quick glance through a list of parent occupations revealed a contact who was able to donate us loads of unwanted cardboard advertisements. The reverse sides were blank and proved to be ideal for the painting and mounting of acrylic paintings.

CLASSROOM DISPLAYS

At the beginning of each school year our classroom appeared to be a depressing place. The echoes of children's voices bounced from wall to wall as the walls looked bare without the colourful displays of children's work. The room looked and felt that it had not been lived in for a while. Within an hour or two of their first arrival, the children were busily engaged in a variety of creative works that soon would have been mounted and displayed over three classroom walls.

Within three weeks of our new school year, our room had already provided a visual impact sufficient to inspire further creative exploration. Already the children showed a growing pride and ownership of their learning space.

"That's my work up there; It's me, it's mine," a child would have told a visiting friend. The expression on her face glowed with pride and satisfaction. With confidence, she had spoken for us all and that helped to reassure us that a rich and colourful year lay ahead in waiting.

THE BACK WALL EASTER 1997

In less than a month, two walls were tastefully covered with artistic achievements. This photograph shows Positive/Negative designs running across the top of the back wall, hats full of written wishes for the coming year, colourful experimentations with chromatography and some written impressions upon life's experiences.

THE ADJOINING WALL EASTER 1997

These photographs were taken at the same time. They showed a display on an adjoining wall that continued the development of Positive/Negative designs using coloured paper squares. Paper Art proved to be an effective starting point for a new year as the colourful creations were quickly completed to enable a swift coverage of the bare walls.

Our classroom was typical of many that were designed and built in the early 1960's. It was a simple weatherboard box like structure that suggested the shape of a rectangular prism. Display boards have since covered two of the walls. The third wall, presumably at the front of the room, boasted a large original chalkboard behind which was a stuffy, narrow cloakroom. A whiteboard has since covered a third of the original chalkboard, the remainder of which was soon to be used as display space. The fourth wall was dominated by window space, recently protected by the addition of vertical blinds. The windows, therefore, were rarely used for display.

THE ADJOINING WALL EASTER 1998

It was interesting to note that as soon as the walls were covered with children's work, the room had prospered from a degree of sound insulation. No longer were we irritated by the shrill of voices bouncing from wall to wall. A sharp reminder of this was deeply felt at the end of each school year as displays were removed. Once again, a bare walled classroom would squeal with an unacceptable noise that would ricochet from wall to wall.

Unnecessary stresses and strains were in part, kept at bay by the manner of or displays and the way we worked together. Our inner contentment was often further enhanced by the soft tones of recorded instrumental music as we creatively worked through each day.

The teacher when he could, played his part in the explorative journeys and his work was also displayed alongside the works of the children. It was part of his learning experience that he should do so. In our classroom we all played our parts as teachers and learners.

THE BACK WALL EASTER 1998

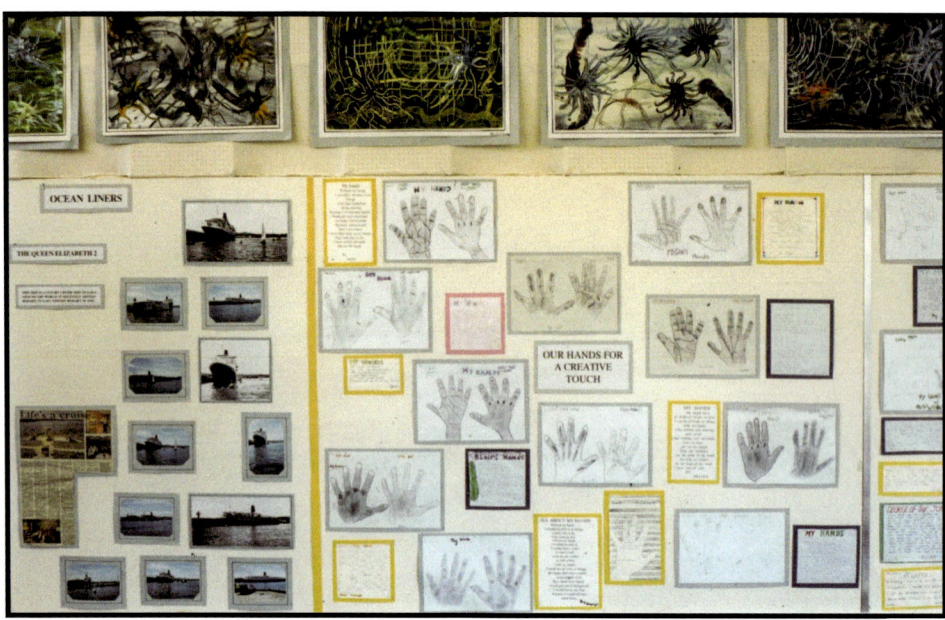

Many teachers preferred to furnish their classroom with attractive displays before the children arrived at the beginning of the school year. It provided the child with a warm welcome. However, I often felt a need for the dramatic and preferred the apparent atmosphere of a stone - cold classroom. We could then speak of the challenge ahead of us and responsibility of building an aesthetic environment together whereby all of us would feel a sense of pride and ownership in our achievements.

These photographs show the mounted Acrylic Abstract paintings, a look at Tall Ships on the Hobart waterfront, and they also show a look at our senses of touch and sight.

We have been looking at the beginning of two consecutive years because we are working in composite classes, that is year 5 and year 6 are working together. Last year's year 5 become this year's year 6. That means a teacher has the children in his care for two consecutive years. It means a teacher has to more than double his repertoire of organised experiences. So, that is why we tried Positive Negative designs in 1997 and in 1998 we tried Acrylic Abstracts. Both artistic explorations are excellent choices for starting a new year.

An added advantage is that the older children know how the classroom works and can act as tutors or assistants in support of their teacher.

Six weeks had passed us by, and the classroom looked great. We all would have appreciated the climb up the hill by admiring the view that lay before our very own eyes. We could then have looked forward with confidence and enthusiasm to our meeting of future challenges.

THE ADJOINING WALL EASTER 1998

The beginning of the school year is crucial for any teacher. First impressions can be long lasting. I hoped that their early days with us would be happy, productive and above all successful. In this particular year I began by introducing the painting of acrylic abstracts. These spectacular paintings were easy to do and ensured success. Those early feelings of success would give us a sufficient tonic to carry each of us through the first weeks of our new school year together

The children's responses to their own experiences of The Tall Ships accompanied the partially completed display about Ships and Seafarers. They were soon followed by research concerning the growing number of 'Cruise Ships'. Investigations into the early, recent, and possible future stories of the Hobart Waterfront were likely to flow on from the initial learning experiences.

The nautical exploits were by no means exclusive to the year's early learning experiences. By Easter two walls were fully laden with work that not only concerned the sea, but other aspects of our curriculum. You may have noticed the illustrated work that considered our eyes and our seeing and our hands and our touching. You might also have noticed a look at our fingerprints and some Maths work concerning Palindromes.

The children had already made their first Clay slab pots for the year. They awaited their first firing in the High School's kiln. The design, making and testing of our Land Yachts was well under way. Above all of that hung our mounted Abstract Acrylic paintings. It was a busy, productive and for the most part a harmonious workplace. We needed the Easter break to catch our breath.

THE SIDE WALL AUGUST 1998

The turnover of our displays was quite frequent. As some were taken down to be housed in their large folders, some more recent work would replace them. The classroom displays were constantly evolving. These photographs were taken late in the second term of the year. They showed a completed display of our work with Trees and Landscapes. It told the story of our journey from the drawing of our first trees to the painting of our first Landscapes with powder paints. Some journeyed further still by responding to an invitation to paint a second landscape of a beauty spot close to Risdon Vale.

Eight children displayed their paintings of an area close to the Risdon Brook Dam. Our display of Trees and landscapes covered the entire side wall of the classroom except a little spot in the left-hand corner. Here, there remained part of our work with Idioms.

THE BACK WALL AUGUST 1998

The back wall at this time was dominated by a display that told the story of our experiments with Colour and the mixing of colours. Note the use of photographs that helped us to explain the steps we had taken on our creative journey. Above the colour wheels, colour lines and the fried eggs, there were our acrylic paintings that depicted our common thoughts and feelings.

We all felt proud of our displays and the time and effort spent was always well worth the trouble. Many of the children seemed to take more care with their work as they knew it would receive great care on completion. The displays made us feel better in ourselves, our self-esteem received a huge boost as we celebrated the joys of our achievements together. If visitors appreciated our displays we felt better still, but if we could feel that we were influencing visitors from other classrooms we would have been ecstatic.

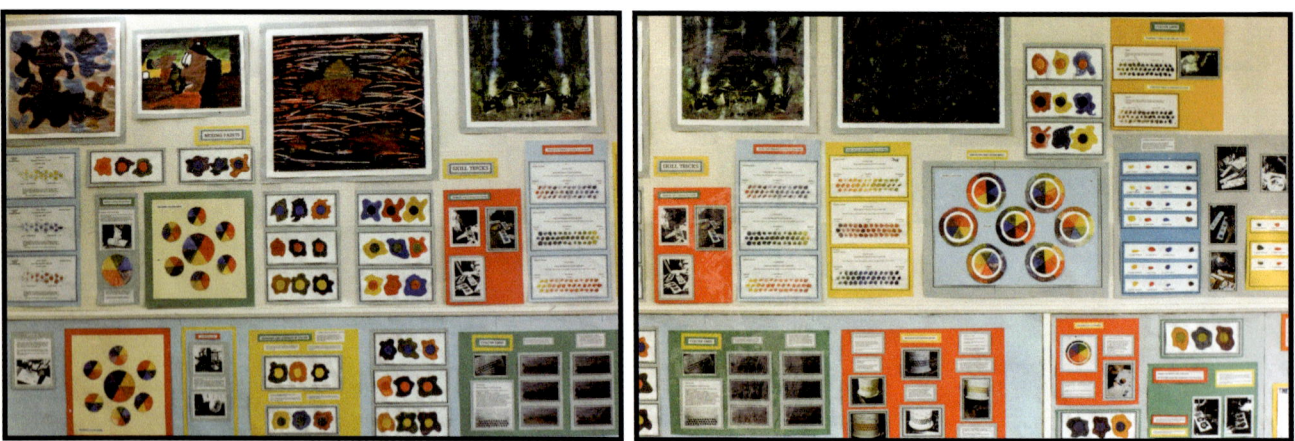

OTHER SCHOOL LOCATIONS SUITABLE FOR DISPLAY

THE CORRIDORS

Adequate display boards were well spread along at least a hundred meters of corridors. They were often dark and gloomy places, and each welcome display would have been enriched by some well-placed spotlights. Corridor displays invited the visitor's interest and after they had been enticed into the home classroom, their praises were very much appreciated by the teacher and children.

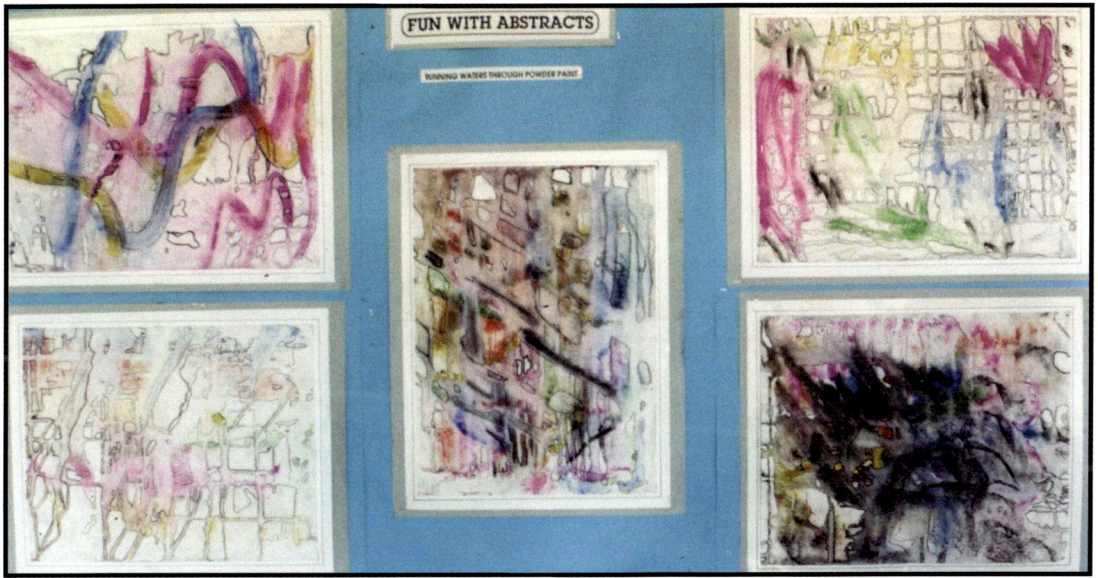

The first photograph showed a corridor display of Abstract paintings created using water, powder paint and a charcoal stick.

THE MULTIPURPOSE ASSEMBLY HALL

This open space was created by the joining together of two classrooms by the removal of a wall, cloakroom, and a blackboard. It was an excellent meeting place. Covering one wall was a wonderful display board. A well-crafted display was well worth the effort and was fully appreciated by the whole school community. The floor was tiled so the space proved to be an excellent location for an Art workshop.

I had planned an after school, Art Workshop for parents, their children, and a few teachers. Part of the set up was a display of children's work completed earlier in the school year. The display concerned the same artistic explorations that the participants were soon to experience. The display was a useful reference point and guide for the children, parents, and the teachers. After the workshop had finished the display was replaced by the work completed by the participants.

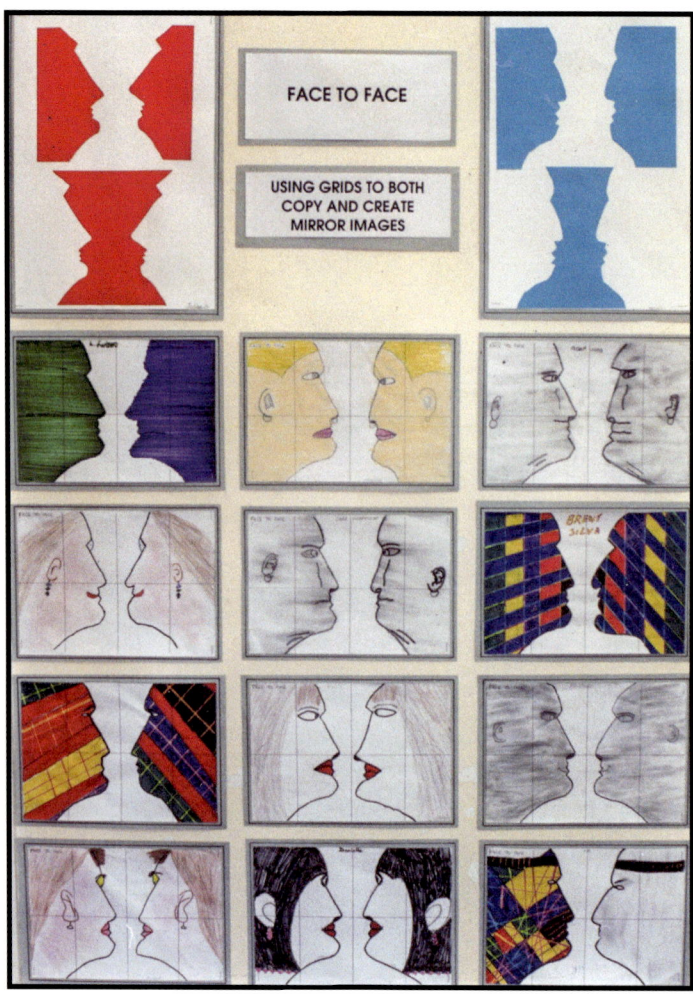

The second showed the use of grids to enable the drawing of a profile of two faces. Each face was the mirror image of the other.

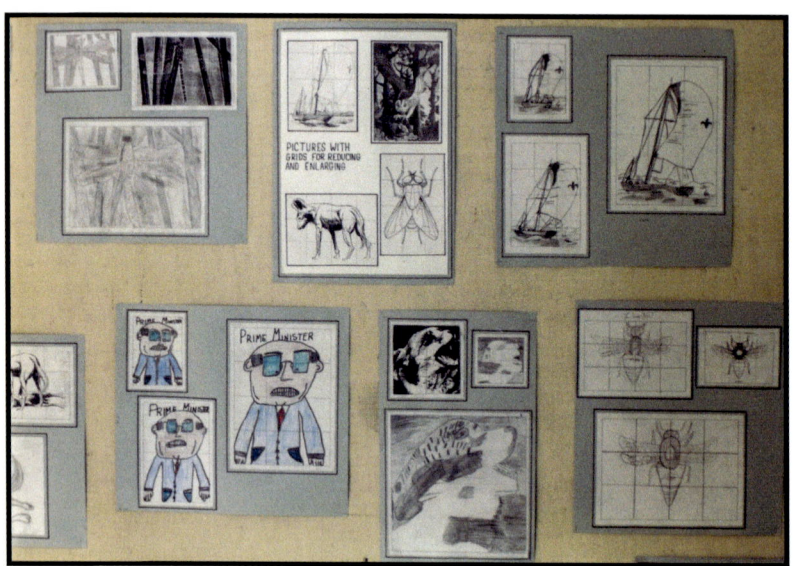

A third once again showed us the use of grids. This time the grids were used to help us enlarge or reduce the size of the image.

The photographs of 'FUN WITH ABSTRACTS' showed our display for our first of three workshops. The display also included photographs and written notes that explained the pathway through our artistic journey.

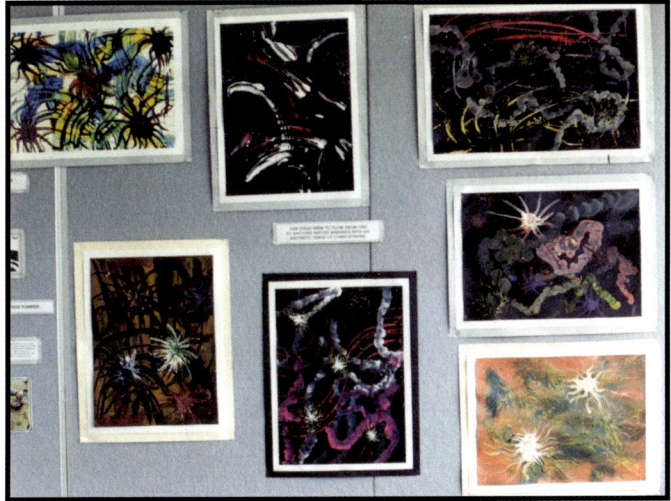 

A SPECIALISED DISPLAY IN THE ACTIVITY ROOM

In earlier days of the 1960's our school would have housed more than twelve hundred children. By 1997, as the housing estate matured, the number of attending children had fallen to a little more than three hundred. One classroom block had been relocated to a more recently established housing estate.

As soon as they became available, empty classrooms provided alternative functions that enriched the nature of our school. Empty rooms were converted to a library, canteen, assembly hall, a music room, an information and technology centre and activity rooms for nearby classrooms. This imaginative use of space created a more ideal learning space for the children and allowed for a greater variety of approaches to learning and teaching. The overcrowded classrooms of yesteryear would have placed severe limitations upon a teacher's approach to teaching and learning. It would have been a nightmare for teachers to manage. I was most thankful to be teaching at Risdon Vale in the mid to late 1990's. An innovation that was most appreciated was that a room adjoining each classroom was converted to an activity room and could be utilised according to a teacher's wishes.

ABSTRACT ACRYLICS ON DISPLAY IN THE ACTIVITY ROOM

Sometimes I would use the wall space of the activity room for a specialised display. After some artistic work had been on display in the classroom, I would rehouse the display in the adjoining activity room. I would add a few delectable extras that explained the story of our creations. I would have displayed some photographs and typed notes that helped to explain the salient features of our artistic journey. The story of our explorations might just inspire teachers and children from other classrooms to have a try themselves. The activity room was also used for woodwork, scientific and mathematical investigations, and as an art studio.

EVOLVING DISPLAYS

As the year progressed our displays were forever changing. By the second term the display clearly reflected the children's progress. The artistic creations were more demanding of their developing skills. We still saw some relatively simple abstracts with powder paint but below that we could see a developing display of our drawings of faces. These early drawings would later lead to the drawing of class portraits.

By the third term a classroom display would appear to be more sophisticated and asking more of their emerging skills. They responded with confidence to the challenges put by their teacher. The mutual trust and support between child with teacher and child with child energised the beating pulse that pumped the life blood of our classroom.

Here on show is our growing understanding of the idea of 'Perspective'. We drew a view of a room looking from one wall to another. Later, we would have tried to draw a view from one corner of the room to another. Below that, there was a display of some mathematical explorations. A small group of children tried to measure the boundary line around the school oval. This would eventually have led us to discover a constant relationship between the diameter and circumference of a circle. Also, there was the display of completed work by of a group of children as they tried to find the area of an irregular shape.

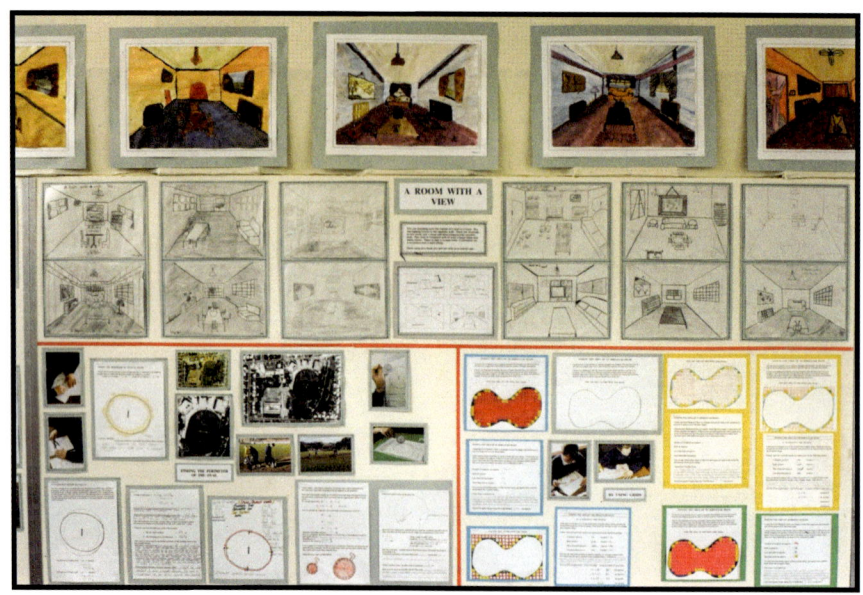

A THEMATIC DISPLAY IN THE CLASSROOM

A VARIETY OF WORK INSPIRED BY A VISIT TO RICHMOND

Our class had spent a lovely day at this rural town rich in convict history. As many tourists do, we first visited the old gaol, which had in the first half of the nineteenth century housed many notorious and unfortunate convicts. We then took to the back streets in search of buildings that had only partially hid some fascinating stories of the past.

That was followed by a slow walk down the main street as we studied many aspects of tourism. After a picnic lunch by the river the children sketched the oldest stone bridge in Australia from several viewpoints.

The three photographs here showed the display of a variety of completed work that was inspired by our visit to Richmond. The Richmond display covered all the back wall of the classroom.

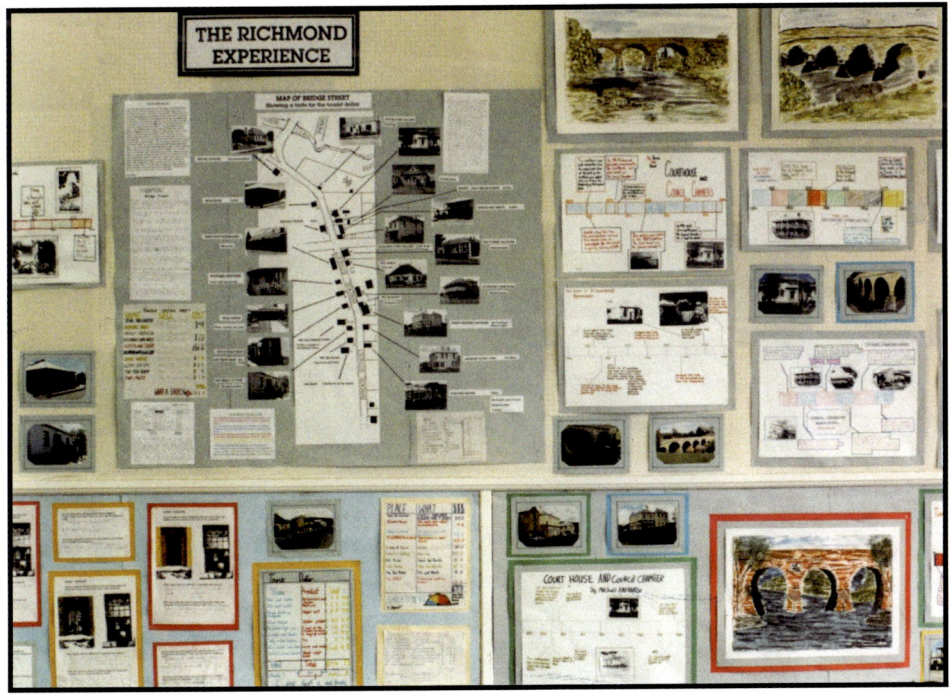

Back at school the children spent a month pursuing activities that built upon our day in Richmond. They constructed Time - Lines that told the story of well-known buildings. Some of them presented a pictorial map of Bridge Street that examined the competitive search for the tourist's dollar. Some sought comparisons between the old stone houses of Richmond and the relatively modern weatherboard houses of Risdon Vale. The sketches of the stone bridge and some of the buildings in Bridge Street were used as platform for further pastel drawings and paintings.

The photographs on this page told the stories of changes in appearance and the functions of some of the old buildings in Richmond.

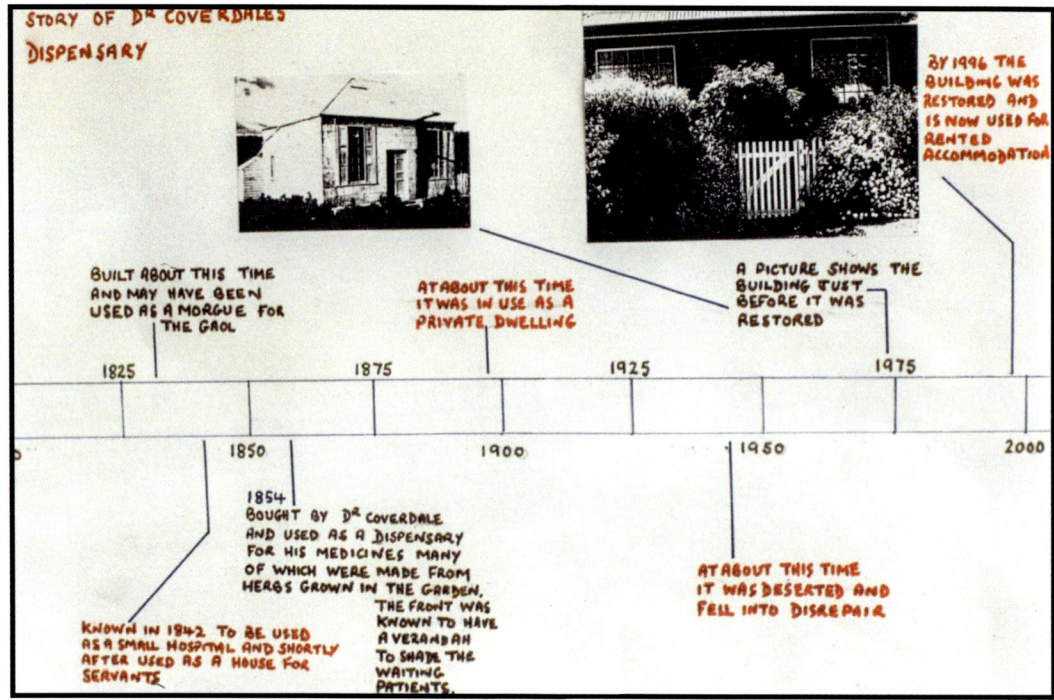

A pictorial map of Bridge Street examined a competitive search for the tourist's dollar.

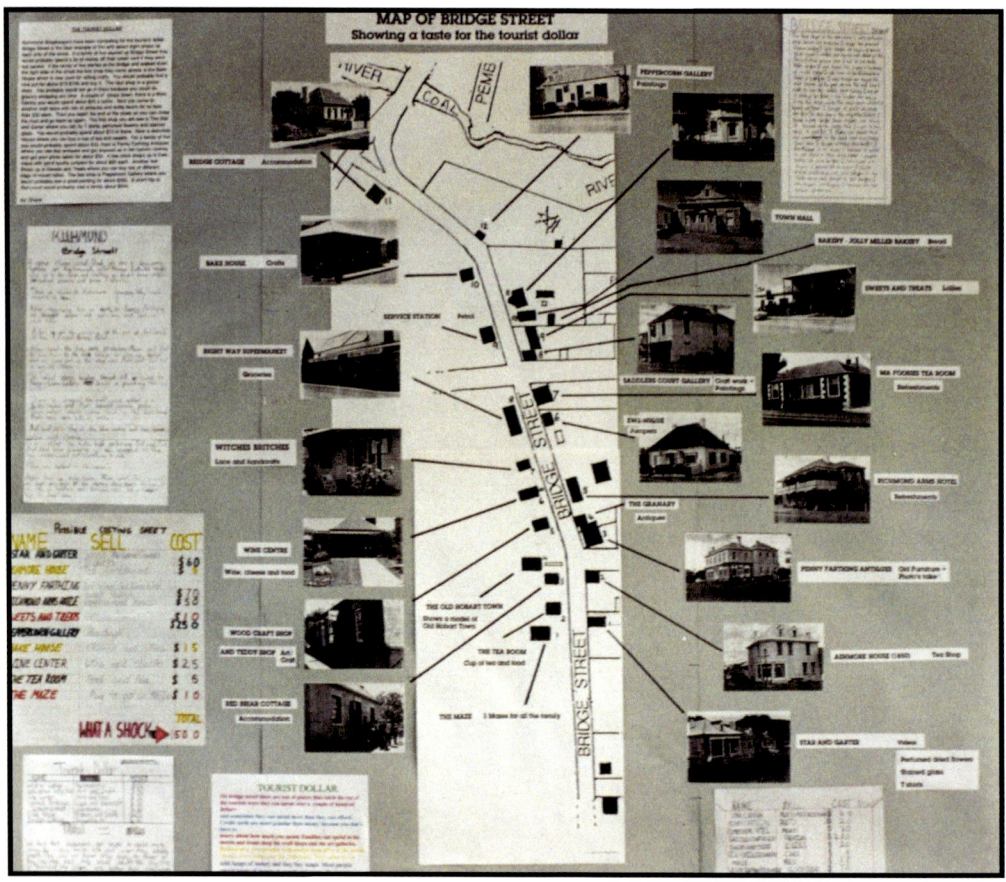

Our Artwork was often an integral part of a complete learning experience that involved many areas of the school curriculum.

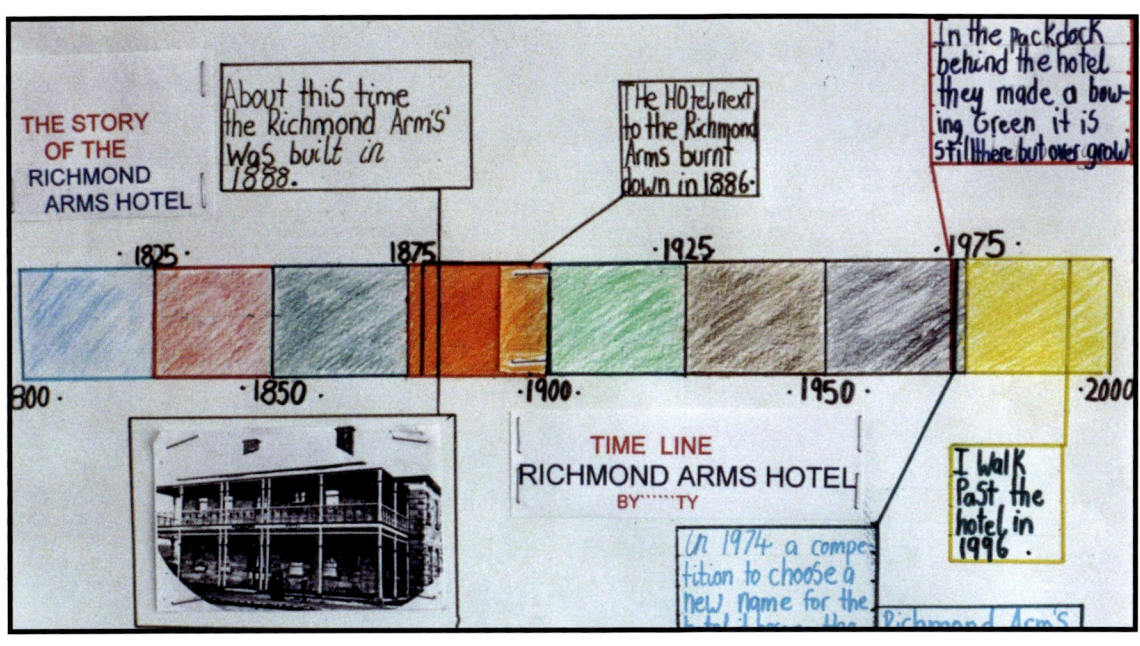

THE STORY
OF THE
RICHMOND
ARMS HOTEL

About this time the Richmond Arms' was built in 1888.

The HOtel next to the Richmond Arms burnt down in 1886.

In the paddock behind the hotel they made a bowling Green, it is still there but over grown

· 1825 ·   1875   · 1925   · 1975 ·

800 ·   · 1850   · 1900 ·   · 1950 ·   · 2000

TIME LINE
RICHMOND ARMS HOTEL
BY """"TY

In 1974 a competition to choose a new name for the hotel. Here the Richmond Acm's

I walk past the hotel in 1996.

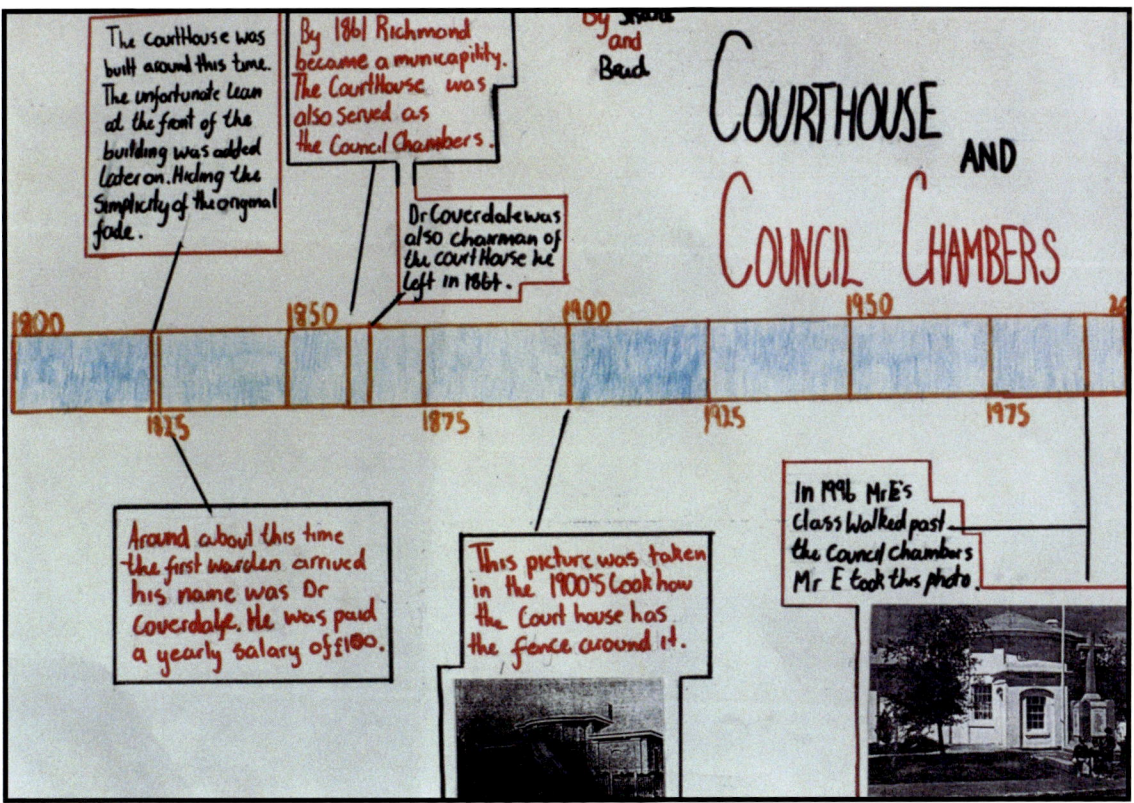

The CourtHouse was built around this time. The unfortunate Lean at the front of the building was added Later on. Hiding the Simplicity of the original fade.

By 1861 Richmond became a municapility. The CourtHouse was also Served as the Council Chambers.

By Shane and Brad

Dr Coverdale was also chairman of the court House he left in 1861.

COURTHOUSE AND COUNCIL CHAMBERS

1900   1850   1900   1950   20

1825   1875   1925   1975

Around about this time the first warden arrived his name was Dr Coverdale. He was paid a yearly salary of £100.

This picture was taken in the 1900's Look how the Court house has the fence around it.

In 1996 Mr E's class Walked past the Council chambers Mr E took this photo.

PICTURE FRAMING

At my previous school, a local picture framer had made and sold to us, some interchangeable picture frames. We used them for the display of children's work in the local community. I thought it would be an excellent idea to develop a similar programme at Risdon Vale. We found a framer in a neighbouring suburb who was willing to supply us a dozen frames that would suit our cause.

I approached some local businesses and found that they would be happy to display framed children's work on their walls. Soon after, the children set about framing the works that were chosen for display.

Cade first mounted his acrylic painting on white cardboard using just enough glue to hold his painting in position. He then turned over the frame face down and unclipped the backing board. He then placed a second sheet of backing paper (black in this case) so that it snuggly fitted into the frame above the glass. The fitting was then checked for a perfect fit. The single mount was then lightly glued over the black backing paper.

After it was lightly pressed, the now double mounted painting was turned over and placed over the glass in the frame. The backing board of the frame was then fitted and secured over the back of the mounted painting.

Cade then viewed his framed painting before he proudly showed it to some admiring observers. Other children soon followed by framing their own paintings. It was time to tell the school about our project at the next assembly.

The picture frames measured about 65cm by 45cm and were of sufficient size to house most of the children's paintings. For our first showing in the community, we had chosen seven framed paintings. The children were delighted to present their paintings to the rest of the school. Emma was chosen to be their speaker and she told the story of the paintings' making in exquisite detail. They were justly proud of their achievements. They thought their work was valued and that they as growing children mattered to people who mattered. I don't think that they had felt before such exhilaration.

ON DISPLAY IN THE COMMUNITY

On the following day they presented their paintings to the local community for display. Like the Beatles crossing Abbey Road they proudly walked to the Risdon Vale shopping centre. The community responses were enthusiastic and very encouraging. The glow on the children's faces as each of their works were received reflected a modest pride, a growing self-esteem, and a genuine belief that they could provide outstanding work.

THE HEALTH CENTRE

Jamie and Chris had their work displayed at the community Health Centre.

THE NEWSAGENCY

Sarah and Adam show their paintings before handing them over to the proprietor. Charles had previously hidden his painting because he had to make sure it was not previously chosen. He wanted to give his painting to Julie.

THE HAIRDRESSERS

Sharyn and Julian presented their paintings to the local hairdresser.

THE NEIGHBOURHOOD CENTRE

Joshua presented his painting to the co-ordinator of the local neighbourhood centre.

THE FIRE STATION

The next day the whole class visited the Fire Station. The firemen and women were very pleased to see us. Lee and Haylee presented their framed paintings to the leading fireman who immediately hung them on a wall. That immediate response impressed the children.

The children were then treated to a tour of the Fire Station before they witnessed a display of firefighting drills. Some children tried on some clothing and some handled firefighting equipment. Some had fun sitting in the fire truck. The local Fire Station was keen to attract junior members to secure the future of an essential community service.

We decided that after a few weeks the framed paintings would be returned to school so that new works by other children could be framed and redistributed throughout the community for display.

The Risdon Vale Community had shown a positive interest in their school. Through our artistic explorations we had stimulated a more positive relationship between the school and its local community. That emerging relationship might well lay the foundation for further growth that would encompass areas that reached far beyond our little world of artistic experiences.

I then prepared a Feedback form for the adult participants in the project. When I visited the premises concerned, not all of them were willing to write their comments on the prepared form. Some thought that they were to be judged in some manner, although they were happy for me to write their verbal comments on the feedback form.

The Health and Neighbourhood Centre came to the rescue and their written comments were typical of all the participants. I decided that the next time our paintings were on show in the community, I would not impose a written evaluation upon them. I would just engage them in worthwhile conversation. I needed their support and had no wish to alienate the good people of Risdon Vale.

It soon became apparent that we had not enough frames to supply the demands of our community. More children wished for their work to be displayed. More community groups and businesses expressed their interest in displaying children's art. We considered raising some money to buy more frames. A parent suggested that the children could market and sell their paintings. They did not like that idea at all. They felt that they just could not let them go forever. They wanted them to be eventually displayed in their own homes as a constant reminder of the magic of their achievements.

I asked the children, who had kindly allowed their paintings to be shown in the community, if they would like to write of their experiences with the project. I thought that their pieces would be a great addition to the photographs that had been already taken and developed.

FEEDBACK FORMS

FEEDBACK FORMS

Risdon Vale Primary School

Heather Road, Risdon Vale 7016
TASMANIA

Principal :- Brendan J. Kelly

Telephone (002)335445
Fax (002 335420

THE PAINTINGS IN THE COMMUNITY PROJECT

AT THE NEIGHBOURHOOD CENTRE

Thankyou for supporting our project by agreeing to hand some of our framed children's paintings on a wall of your premises. Could you please take a moment to complete this Feedback Form as we would sincerely value your comments.

Have you enjoyed displaying the paintings? *very much, hope the idea continues.*

Did you experience any difficulties in displaying the paintings? *No.*

Did the display encourage responses by visitors to your premises? *yes. Visitors were surprised at times to find the work was completed by children, as they look quite professional*

Could you please summarise some typical responses? *The paintings all look professional. It lovely to see the children's work on display. Some of the older community of Risdon Vale don't often get a chance to see the children's work. I know a lot of them were impressed.*

Has your display provided good publicity for your Business? and our school? In what way? *It has helped having them on display as it gives us a chance to see the standard of work being produced. It would be good if the Risdon Vale Art group could have an exhibition of their works at the school, side by side with the*

Have you any suggestions to make regarding the continuation of our project? *Children I would like to see the project continue & maybe include the Fire Brigade, 50 & overs and even some of the church groups.*

Would you like to receive some replacement paintings in the near future? *Yes.*

Thankyou so much for taking the time to fill in this Feed Back Form.

THE PAINTINGS IN THE COMMUNITY PROJECT

AT THE HEALTH CENTRE

Thankyou for supporting our project by agreeing to hand some of our framed children's paintings on a wall of your premises. Could you please take a moment to complete this Feedback Form as we would sincerely value your comments.

Have you enjoyed displaying the paintings? *yes*

Did you experience any difficulties in displaying the paintings? *no*

Did the display encourage responses by visitors to your premises? *yes it has. People have been very impressed with the high standard.*

Could you please summarise some typical responses? *Excellent work. surprise at the age of the students that did them.*

Has your display provided good publicity for your Business? and our school? In what way? *People are pleased with the standard of the artwork turned out by the school.*

Have you any suggestions to make regarding the continuation of our project? *Special projects like this need to be highlighted to express the positives of the young people of Risdon Vale*

Would you like to receive some replacement paintings in the near future? *yes - very mu*

Thankyou so much for taking the time to fill in this Feed Back Form.

David Esling
Teacher

Forwarded through
Brendan J. Kelly
Principal   *Brendan J. Kelly*

This was the first of many community displays of our children's artwork. The second term saw a display of our portrait drawings. The third term followed with a display of our landscape paintings of the Risdon Brook Dam. For subsequent terms and years, we found no difficulty in finding children's artwork, as nearly all the children aspired to having their work chosen for community display.

Children's written comments about the community displays

BOY 1

I just couldn't believe it believe it when MrE asked me if I would like my artwork to be displayed in the community. Julian helped me mount and frame it and then I had to show it to the rest of the school in the assembly hall. I felt real nervous standing in front of everyone. Along with some other kids we went to the shopping centre. I gave my painting to Julie at the newsagents. She liked my painting very much and I liked her. This has been one of my best days at school ever. It feels just great.

BOY 2

It was great to be asked to display my painting at the shopping centre. I never thought that one of my paintings would be chosen as I thought I was one of the dumb ones. I felt real proud as we walked to the Health Centre. I felt great when I gave my painting to one of the people there. She said that might painting looked real nice and she would hang it up in a special place. We are back at school now and I can't wait to do it all over again.

Although it was early in the school year, two of the boys had recently passed their twelfth birthday. They were in their second year of our composite class of year 5 and year 6 students. When they began their time with us a little more than a year ago, they were barely literate and numerate. Numbers, letters, and words to them appeared to rise through a meaningless misty, mazy fog that carried little meaning. We spent ages with the help of a supporting teacher to build up their understanding of numbers, letters, and words to reach a very basic standard in computation, reading and writing. If we could find appropriate stimuli to give them a genuine need to want to read, write and be numerate then we would be well on course to meet our goals. Our emphasis on creative explorations helped enormously to boost their self-esteem, confidence, articulation, social skills, and a sense of belonging in a learning environment that mattered to them. On being asked to do so, these two boys were very keen to express their written thoughts and feelings about the lending of their paintings to members of the Risdon Vale community. With caring support these two boys were able to write of such experiences without the fear of spelling or grammatical errors. They had fun exploring their language to find the best way to express the salient features of an experience that mattered so much to them. When they read their pieces to some other children they did so with so much enthusiasm and joyful expression that the listener would have thought them to be skilled readers and writers. Without the artistic experience in the first place, they would have been unable to write anything of substance enough to entice the interest of a reader or listener.

A FINALE ON DISPLAY

I liked to keep a photographic record of all my creative work with the children. By the time I left Risdon Vale in September 2000 I had filled two large photo albums with pictures and written notes of my experiences. They certainly kept my memories alive well into my ageing years, but more important for me was that they were a useful guide for me when I was to repeat any of the artistic explorations at school. The albums were both my records and preparations for future endeavours. All I had to do was read of my previous experience, find my starting point and off we would go. It was interesting to find that whenever an exploration was repeated a couple of years later the outcome would always be a little different.

This book would never have been written had it not been for my two albums of notes and photographs. The albums were kept in the classroom and the children knew where to find them. We often had visitors to our classroom and the children were always keen to show them around our various exhibits. The child guides would often bring out the two albums and show my records to friends and relatives. They loved to point out photographs of their previous work that no longer covered the classroom walls.

"Look Grandpa, that's me, and that's one of my paintings," Emma would have said.

THE RISDON VALE ART GROUP

A child's mother visited our classroom recently and was keen to show me one of her oil paintings. She was obviously thrilled with her work, and she further enjoyed the supportive praise received from both the teacher and the children. She then told me that she was a member of the local community art group that met once a week at the Neighbourhood Centre.

A keener awareness of the Art group's existence followed by my watching them paint a mural on an aboriginal theme on one of the walls of the infant block. Carol Rodwell, "Caz" was their leader of a band of about a dozen mothers who happily co-operated as a team in the painting of the mural. Their work generated considerable interest from a growing lunchtime audience of children.

The Neighbourhood Centre employed a paid coordinator who planned and implemented several services and courses for people of Risdon Vale. There were courses for the building of self-esteem, parenting issues, and of course there was the Art group. The Centre also assisted in the filling in of welfare forms, C. V's, and applications for employment. If necessary, they organised food parcels for the most in need.

The Art group consisted of about a dozen mothers and grandmothers who pursued several artistic pleasures under the capable leadership of Caz Rodwell. A visit was arranged for me to witness the Art group in action in a room at the Centre. I was immediately impressed by the lovely atmosphere as the members of the group worked together, each in support of the other.

"Could I please bring a small group of children to witness this group in action?" asked MrE.

"Of course, you can. We were hoping that you would ask us that," Caz replied.

STILL LIFE

In the Centre's art room, there was an arrangement of Irises in a vase, a glass bottle, jug, and some fruit.

The painters used the arrangement as a source of reference and inspiration. Some painted all the objects as they saw them but most of them seemed to paint a selected few on an imaginary surface. They felt free to paint the subject as they wished. Back at school the children would have sat around a Still Life arrangement and encouraged to draw what they actually saw.

'Caz' felt quite at ease in demonstrating a point by brushing oil paint onto a participant's canvass. Oil paints were user friendly in that some brushed paint could easily be covered over by another brush of oil paint. Back at school the primary teacher would not have touched the children's work for fear of removing the ownership of the work from the child.

It was interesting to note that the mothers of three of the children in our class, Sarah, Luke, and Adrian, were members of the Risdon Vale Art group.

Sarah's mother explains to Emma how she was going to continue with her painting

They all enjoyed their weekly meetings as each of them in their own way realized that their gatherings offered so much more than the joy and pride on completing a painting,

A mother kept her watchful eye on the Still Life arrangement. Most of the painters kept their distance from the display thus supporting a free and expressive interpretation. Mutual support and encouragement were very much in evidence and sighs of frustration were rarely noticed. There seemed to be little evidence of a fear of failure as they enthusiastically approached their tasks. They had obviously been working together for some time.

A simple chalk outline over a painted background provided a guide for the painting of her Still Life objects.

Some others preferred to simply paint the outlines using a small brush.

I had an interesting conversation with 'Caz' and the coordinator of the Neighbourhood Centre Anne Harrison after our first visit to see the Risdon Vale Art group in action. They revealed that it was not their intention to develop artists of local significance but rather to use 'Art' to boost their self-esteem and further develop their socially interactive skills. Some members of the group over a few years had developed the necessary social skills and confidence to seek and achieve employment in the work force.

I was told that one member of the group had progressed to study at a city ART school.

"But that's not what we are all about," they stressed. "We, through artistic expression wish to lift their self - esteem, their confidence, social skills and their wellness of being."

"You are so right," MrE replied. "I have been trying to do just that while I have been teaching at the Primary School. Perhaps your Art group might like to visit our classroom soon?"

A second visit with a different group of children revealed the wonderful progress the Art group had made with their Still Life paintings. The children were impressed by their skills and techniques in adding detail to their backgrounds. They also liked the variety of colour tones used to convey light shining on bottles, jugs, and vases.

Sarah was watching in admiration as her mother added the finishing touches to her Still Life painting "Irises"

"Can we try some Still Life with oil paints MrE?"

"We could, but first I think we should try painting Still Life with thick Acrylic paints. Perhaps after that we could try oil paints. I have never ever used oil paints before."

"That shouldn't stop you MrE," said Sarah. "You have often said you have never done this before and just did it. I want to try it now."

"Well, you could try joining the Risdon Vale Art group," he said with a smile.

"Oh MrE, you are teasing me, you know they only meet in school times."

Every second year, the ART group held an exhibition of their work in neighbouring community halls so that the responses from a wider audience could be felt and appreciated.

Caz and her group of painters had exceeded their expectations. Their works looked wonderful but of far greater significance, was the painters' growth in confidence, self-esteem and the collaborative social skills that helped so much to emphasise the necessity of this special group's existence.

The paintings were finally completed and displayed in the best possible manner. Cade really liked this painting of "Irises" He was fascinated by the uneven folds of the foreground material that held the vase in place.

THE RISDON VALE ART GROUP VISITS OUR CLASSROOM

Caz and the members of the Risdon Vale Art group were invited to witness the artistic life of our classroom. This time the children controlled the sharing of ideas that covered a wide range of artistic experiences.

The visitors were enthralled by a display of the children's first attempts to paint simple landscapes. They admired the simple steps taken that would have ensured success.

They enjoyed our look at the mixing of colours and the fun we had earlier experienced with painting abstracts.

They enjoyed looking at the photographic record of our presentation of framed paintings by the children to the business and service centres around Risdon Vale.

They too, were excited about the mysteries of mixing the colour "Brown". They then witnessed a group of children make up a 'Brown' by mixing up a combination of Primary Colours. They had a share of the children's pleasure on discovering 'Brown' by mixing all the Secondary Colours.

The group's first visit to our classroom had proved to be a great success and we all agreed it would be a wonderful idea to continue with a reciprocal cycle of meetings. Perhaps a creative consequence might be the planning of several shared learning experiences both in the school and in the community.

We decided to work towards a shared public exhibition of our creative works at some time in the following year. We also discussed the possibility of the Art group using some of the available space in the school. A vacant classroom would help the group expand their numbers for they already had a long list of prospective members. Perhaps the school could open its doors for evening classes in an activity room or the under used assembly hall. Our opportunities seemed endless and all we had to do was open the doors of our hearts and minds and together with confidence and purpose, our imaginative dreams could turn into reality.

THE MURALS

The Risdon Vale Art group earned an enviable reputation for the painting of Murals on vacant wall spaces within the community. They began with the Sports Pavilion and the local bus stop. In 1996 they were invited by the school management committee to paint some murals around the school. They began with a mural that spoke of aboriginal culture and followed that by a mural that covered three walls of the infant block.

A WALL SPACE

Several children submitted ideas for a "Space" theme, many of which were incorporated into the painting by the Art group.

Before the murals were painted the walls were favourite places for graffiti lovers. It was noted with appreciation that after the murals were painted, the walls were no longer targets for such abuse.

SPACE IN A WALL

One lunch time I joined a group of young children looking at the recently painted mural on the walls of the infant block.

"It looks great, doesn't it?" asked MrE "What do you like most of all?"

"I like the planets and the rockets," replied one of them.

A WALL IN SPACE

"I think I like the stars because they twinkle at night time."

"I like the way the planets have faces." said another.

"The moon seems to be crying. I wonder why?" asked the teacher.

"I know, he's crying 'cause he's lost in space," replied a little boy in grade 1 as he took off in his space rocket.

Unfortunately for us, a nasty surprise lay in waiting.

During the lunch break on September 29th, 1997, we were stunned by the shrieks of sirens.

"FIRE!!"
"FIRE!!"
"FIRE!!"

The music room had caught on fire and for fifteen minutes it was burning out of control. Teachers quickly grabbed the registers from their classrooms, checked to see that there were no children inside and ushered every child they could see to the meeting place near the oval.

It was indeed fortunate that everyone was outside during this lunch break as the weather was fine. The Risdon Vale Fire Brigade was the first on the scene and quickly had their hoses dowsing the fire. They were soon assisted by two other Brigades and the fire was put out within forty minutes.

The following week saw the arrival of the demolition squad. Within a week an excavator had cleared the site. It was so sad to see the charred remains of musical instruments scooped up and dropped into skip bins. That really emphasised our sense of loss. By the Friday of that week all that remained of the music room was a flattened space that was readied to be covered with asphalt. A haven for the Arts was lost.

Since ample space remained within the school, the lost building was not replaced. The music room was rehoused in a vacant classroom. The vacant space was asphalted, and a wall was built of large concrete slabs to enclose the quadrangle. Another wall was built adjacent to it at 90 degrees. On top of the walls wire netting was placed for reasons of security. It began to look like a prison. The ugly looking walls intruded upon the aesthetic nature of our school.

Like knights in shining armour, The Risdon Vale Art group came to the rescue. The local community felt and shared the loss with the school and covered some of the expenses required to paint a mural on the recently built wall.

This time, the children in our class were involved in the painting of it. The children and the community shared the loss, and it was appropriate that they, side by side, would be actively involved in the project. It was part of the healing process. Each afternoon a group of six children were released to join the art group in the painting of a "Secret Garden."

Some members of the Art group painted a background. It was a hot day and they frequently stopped for a rest and a chat.

The first group of children had arrived, and Caz discussed with them the features that should appear in a secret garden. Some outlines were then chalked in over the background. Under Caz's watchful eye the children then enriched the background by adding varying tones of colour. Then they began to add detail to the background.

After the sunflowers had been chalked in over the background three boys had begun to paint the leaves. The black circle above them is the background over which the petals of the sunflower will be painted.

THE SUNFLOWERS

Slowly but surely, the mural depicting a secret garden began to take shape. The outline of a white fence was drawn with chalk, and painted in. Shrubs and flowers were drawn and painted in front of the fence thus breaking the fence lines for added interest. The petals of the sunflowers were painted in. The smiling faces of the sunflowers did not all need to look in the same direction.

THE WHITE FENCE AND GATE

Insects such as butterflies and bees made a timely appearance as they sought the nectar from an abundance of flowers.

It was a wonderful sight to witness the mothers and children working together. All in need of each other to find a soothing antidote for the sadness of losing the music room. They all knew that it had to be beautiful as indeed it was clearly going to be so.

The children loved being involved in the production of a Secret Garden.

"I will be both sad and glad when we have finished this lovely mural," said Sharyn. "I will be sad because we will be no longer out here painting it. I will be glad because it looks so nice and that we did some of the painting."

"I agree," added Melinda. "It looks so much better than that horrible grey wall."

Soon enough the finishing touches were applied. Emma painted a butterfly; Chris added a touch to some distant trees, whilst Danielle tidied up the appearance of the front fence.

Our Secret Garden was finally completed, and the gate was opened. Melinda and Sharyn were there to greet us and take us for a walk inside. Among the shrubs and blooms there buzzed and crawled a host of insects.

Once inside the secret garden....... "Sh! ..." We had to be quiet. If we listened carefully, we could hear the distant sounds of recorders and guitars softly blending with the hum of insects and wafted birdsong.

A PANAORAMIC VIEW OF OUR SECRET GARDEN

THE TREE OF FRIENDSHIP

There was another dull looking blank wall adjacent to the Secret Garden. The Risdon Vale Art group had a mural planned for that one too. This time they invited children from another class to be their assistants. They decided to paint a "Friendship Tree". The fruit of the tree was the - happy smiling faces of children as they looked down to receive the grasping hands of children from all over the world.

The hands that were seeking friendship were painted in several colours to convey the need for multi-racial friendship across the globe. The faces of the children were also multicolored providing us with a hint of some previous progress with racial harmony.

If you look closely at the tree trunk you might be able to find another face. Perhaps it might be "Mother Nature," keeping an eye on us all and reminding us to keep the world at peace with harmony amongst all its people.

BEYOND THE CLASSROOM WALLS

THE EXTENSION OF OUR LEARNING ENVIRONMENT

By the end of the first term several of our artistic displays had attracted the interest of children, parents, and teachers. Some children from neighbouring classrooms wished to partake a share of our artistic explorations. Some of them, as part of a reward system, had been permitted to spend an afternoon in our classroom. Undoubtedly, they would have been guided towards such activities by one of our capable class child tutors. Some of our child tutors had been invited into other classrooms to lead a small group of children through an artistic exploration. We were happy to do this as we dearly wished to share and spread our more successful approaches. However, the frequencies of such events were sporadic and their effects, although useful, were hardly long lasting. I discussed the matter with a few interested teachers and then we made some plans for further action and interaction.

Here follows an outline for our plans for consideration.

FORM AN ART GROUP

We began with three or four teachers forming a discussion group who shared a common interest in ART in EDUCATION.

We met in each other's classrooms to share our experiences and approaches to teaching and learning with Art. We sought means of spreading sound artistic practice throughout the whole school community. We discussed a more meaningful and interactive relationship with the local High School's ART Department. A high school art teacher could join our Art group or lead us into an Art Workshop. An outcome of further interaction might well lead us towards some form of purposeful continuity of practice from Primary to High School.

We could embrace a more realistic and effective community involvement with the school. This might include the following strategies,

(a) A register of community expertise.
    We could survey the interest and expertise of both parents and community members. Some of them could be active leaders of small groups of creative children. Costs could be shared by the school and the Neighbourhood centre.

(b) Parents as members of the School Management Council.

Encourage two or three parents known to be interested in the 'Arts' to join the School Management Council. This might ensure that the 'Arts' are properly budgeted for in a balanced educative environment.

COPIES OF LETTERS TO PARENTS

(c) The Organization of Art Workshops.

These artistic workshops could be for Parents, their children, and Teachers. We could all profit by learning together and thus speeding up the flow of ideas across the school, through to our homes and into the community.

AN EXAMPLE OF AN ART WORKSHOP FOR TEACHERS, PARENTS AND THEIR CHILDREN

First, we had to choose some artistic explorations that were likely to be successful and be familiar with children who would act as child tutors. We also had to keep in mind that age range of the participants would likely be from 8 yrs. to 50 yrs.

We chose "FUN WITH ABSTRACTS" as an explorative theme for our first workshop. We then had to invite the participation of those with whom we wished to share the experience. We also had to seek parental permission for the participating child tutors. Their role as tutors would provide a vital key to the success of our workshop.

THE SET UP

The location for our workshop was to be "The Open Room". This assembly area was once two classrooms that has since been converted into a large multi-purpose facility. The floor was ideally tiled and housed a canteen at one end.

We chose the two styles of Abstracts that the children would have previously experienced and set up a display of their work to act as useful reference point for our participants in the workshop.

MAP OF WORKSHOP LOCATION SHOWING LEARNING CENTRES

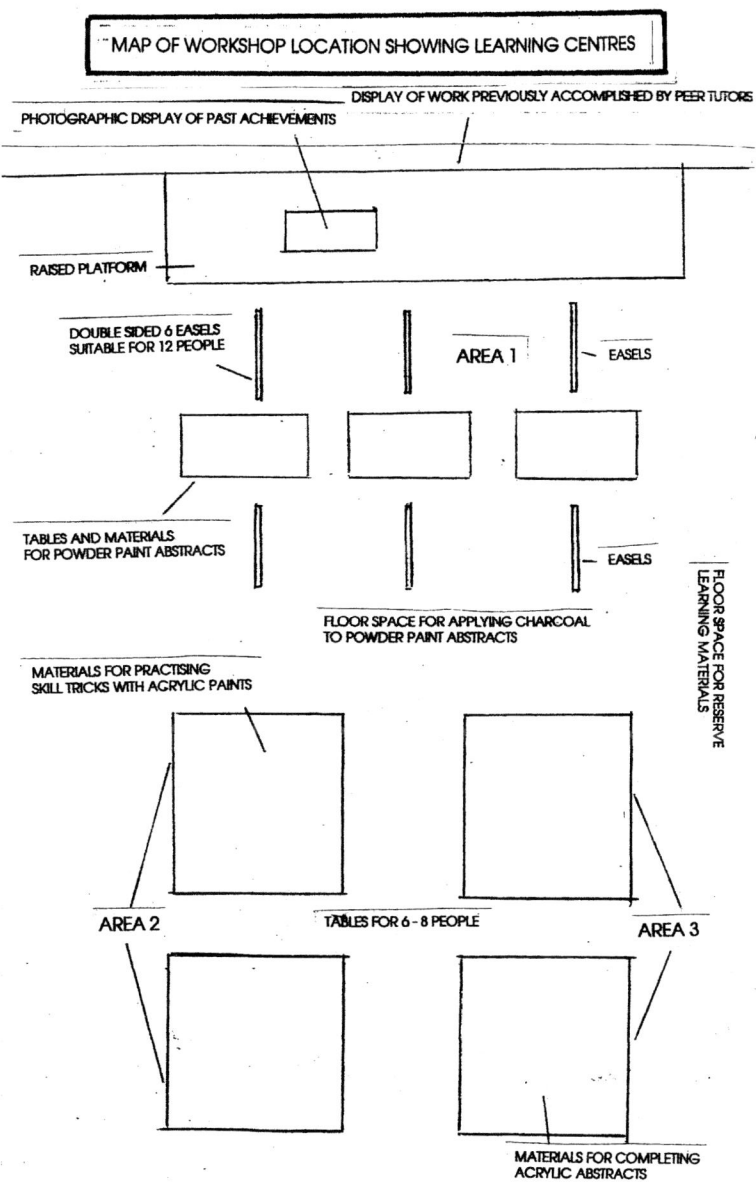

MAP OF WORKSHOP LOCATION SHOWING LEARNING CENTRES

DISPLAY OF WORK PREVIOUSLY ACCOMPLISHED BY PEER TUTORS

PHOTOGRAPHIC DISPLAY OF PAST ACHIEVEMENTS

RAISED PLATFORM

DOUBLE SIDED 6 EASELS
SUITABLE FOR 12 PEOPLE

AREA 1   EASELS

TABLES AND MATERIALS
FOR POWDER PAINT ABSTRACTS

EASELS

FLOOR SPACE FOR APPLYING CHARCOAL
TO POWDER PAINT ABSTRACTS

FLOOR SPACE FOR RESERVE
LEARNING MATERIALS

MATERIALS FOR PRACTISING
SKILL TRICKS WITH ACRYLIC PAINTS

AREA 2   TABLES FOR 6 - 8 PEOPLE   AREA 3

MATERIALS FOR COMPLETING
ACRYLIC ABSTRACTS

FUN WITH ABSTRACTS

PARTICIPANTS

10 PARENTS WITH ONE CHILD

4 TEACHERS AND 6 CHILD TUTORS

TOTAL 30

PREPARATION

A display of children's previous work provided us with a useful reference and guide for our emerging workshop paintings.

SETTING UP THE WORKSPACES

RUNNING WATER THROUGH POWDER PAINTS

MATERIALS NEEDED

Easels, shiny litho paper or white sheets of thin cardboard and Masking Tape

On each of the two small tables between each easel Six containers of powder paint, four large house paint brushes 5cm +, two large containers of water (large enough to hold the large house paint brushes) sponges and cloth wipes.

For the second phase we would need some charcoal sticks on standby.

SKILL TRICKS WITH ACRYLICS

TEASING, TWIRLING AND ROLLING BRUSHES THROUGH PAINT

Materials Needed

Plastic containers of acrylic paints. Large round bristle brushes, Plastic forks, and spoons, Litho paper A4 size, Cloth wipes and Sponges.

PAINTING ACRYLICS OVER AN ACRYLIC BACKGROUND

Materials Needed

Plastic plates of Acrylic Paints, Cardboard combs, large house paint brushes, large round bristle brushes, Icy pole sticks, Plastic spoons and forks, Sheets of white cardboard, Cloth wipes and Sponges.

THE PLAN INTO ACTION

After an hour and a half all the participants should have completed two paintings.

1. Powder Paint Abstracts. Charcoal would later have been added after the powder paints were dry.
2. Acrylic Abstracts with some skill tricks superimposed over a combed background here]]

THE PROCEDURE

IN AREA ONE

After a warm welcome, Mr E demonstrated to everyone the necessary starting points for the Abstract Powder Paintings; The wash, the running paint, and the creation of tide marks by using saturated house paint brushes.

Emma a child tutor, explained to a teacher the value of rotating the paper so that the paint ran in variable directions.

IN AREA TWO

MrE then quickly moved over to Area two and demonstrated some simple skill tricks with acrylic paint that would be much in need later; the teasing out of droplets of paint with an icy pole stick or twisting and turning and rolling bristle brushes through acrylic paint.

A teacher is supporting a fellow teacher.

The two demonstrations would have only taken about fifteen minutes before the participants were invited to work in area 'One' or 'Two'. After about twenty minutes they would have swapped places from one working area to the other. During this period MrE would have been active in providing support and encouragement to the children, their parents, and the teachers. Mr E was very much aware of the varied and meaningful interactions that were taking place – child supporting child, child encouraging a teacher, child supporting a parent, teacher alongside a parent and so on, all accepting each other as equals by sharing a common learning experience. The unique learning experience sang with such melodic harmony.

A child tutor is lending support to a parent.

Two mothers and children together practicing acrylic skill tricks.

THE ACRYLIC PAINTINGS IN AREA 3

After about forty-five minutes we all moved into Area 3. The creation of an interesting background was demonstrated and that was followed by the superimposing of the recently acquired skill tricks. Our highly motivated participants then proceeded with their own acrylic paintings each of them feeling safe in the knowledge that mutual support was readily forthcoming. It was a rare joy to witness such unforgettable harmony in such a unique learning environment.

Two teachers applied a second background over the top of the first one. Sarah was very busy supporting both as they dragged their cardboard combs to reveal parts of the first background.

BACK IN AREA 1

After a further half hour, the group was invited back to AREA 1. The water runs of powder paints would have dried by then. Mr E demonstrated the use of charcoal sticks to accentuate the line and shape of some of the tide marks left by running water. The learning group naturally followed by charcoaling their own paintings.

Cade in his role of tutor discussed the application of charcoal with a teacher and some parents. He even found time to paint one himself.

FINISHING OFF

The music of Vivaldi had stopped thus indicating that the allotted time for our workshop had come to end. The hour and a half had flown by. Our works of art were left to dry at one end of the room. We cleaned up and chatted about the experience and highlighted significant events. We all agreed that the workshop had been a great success and a sequel should be planned for later in the school year.

"Mr E, why did you play that lovely music while we were painting?" he was asked.

"There are a lot of good reasons. First, I played a cassette that lasted for an hour and a half. That was my timing piece. I also like music in the background as it makes me feel good, it energises and inspires me. It also helps us to keep the working noise at an acceptable level. However, my most significant reason is this. Music and Art to me are inseparable. They are an intrinsic part of the human existence and have been so for centuries. The music of Vivaldi reminds me of this. His music is over three hundred years old. It was played before white men settled at Risdon Cove. Ever since mankind has lived on this planet he has used 'ART' to tell his story, to express his thoughts and feelings, his hopes, and aspirations. Let us hope that it will remain to be so for centuries to come."

He continued by telling them that their works would be left to dry overnight.

"Tomorrow, I will house them on the floor of the activity room next to our classroom. You can visit us and finish off your charcoaling on any afternoon this week. Some of you might like to add some estapol to your acrylic paintings. The children would be pleased to guide you through that. We shall then find a suitable location to display your wonderful paintings. Before you all go could you take this form of review and return it to me as soon as possible. Thank you all. It has been a wonderful evening."

BACK IN THE CLASSROOM

By the following day the paintings were dry and moved to the activity room next to our classroom. Teachers, mothers, and children from other classes found time to visit us in the afternoons. Estapol was brushed over the acrylic paintings providing us with a more vivid colour and sheen. Some finished the charcoaling of their powder paintings. The child tutors were still keen to offer their support. It was as if the workshop had been extended. They all felt a need to return to the artistic experience. They were not ready to let it sink back into the mingled memories of time passed.

A feedback form was designed to gather support and advice for future art workshops.

ART WORKSHOP FEEDBACK FORM

ART WORKSHOP FEEDBACK FORM ·

Thank you very much for participating in the recent Workshop Fun with Abstracts .

Could you please take a moment to fill in this feedback form as the information you provide may help to ensure the success of future Workshops.

PARTICIPATOR S ROLE
     Tick Appropriate box

Parent with Child	☐
Teacher	☐
Child as Tutor	☐

COULD YOU COMMENT BRIEFLY ON THE FOLLOWING:

The suitability of the location _____

_____

The Organisation of Learning Space, Materials and Experiences

_____

The Use of Children as Tutors _____

_____

_____

The Learning experiences themselves

The Powder Paint and Charcoal   The Acrylic Abstracts

A magic moment for me was   Next time I would like to

Any advice for Mr. E. or other relevant comments

_____   Signed...
                                          Thanking you so much for your t
_____   David Esling.

- 278 -

A GATHERING OF IMPRESSIONS

THE SUITABILITY OF THE LOCATION

Great easy to find!

PARENT WITH CHILD

Great, plenty of room to move. The Lino floor made the cleaning up much easier.

CHILD AS TUTOR

It was good because it is the biggest space in the school and there's room to move.

TEACHER

Very suitable - but what about when it's carpeted?
Room to move about & look at what others were doing & not interfere, also plenty of light.

THE ORGANISATION OF LEARNING SPACE, MATERIALS AND EXPERIENCES

PARENT WITH CHILD

I found the set up easy to move around in,
The organisation of space was excellent & the use of material was extremely generous

CHILD AS TUTOR

It was very thought out
Well defined areas materials readily available & gradation of experience

TEACHER

Well organised - sufficient space to work comfortably and easy access & movement from one activity to another.

THE USE OF CHILDREN AS TUTORS

PARENT WITH CHILD

Very good. They were helpful and very mature. I was pleased that they asked us if we wanted help, we didn't have to ask them for help.
All the children were helpful & made things a lot easier.

CHILD AS TUTOR

It was good because kids understood other kids. The adults understood what we were telling them because we know what we were doing

TEACHER

Great to be in the "other" position although rarely is there a great divide. The children were polite encouraging & helpful.

Excellent - we all felt like equals!

THE LEARNING EXPERIENCES

PARENT WITH CHILD

Very enjoyable. I was surprised that something so simple could look so good.

I was surprised how such simple ideas made such interesting & unusual pieces.

I kept adding to it and over did it! My son's was great.

I did not realise how easy it was to achieve something. I always thought art was something you had to be talented at.

A WALK IN THE GALLERY

THE CHILDREN

Megan W 11

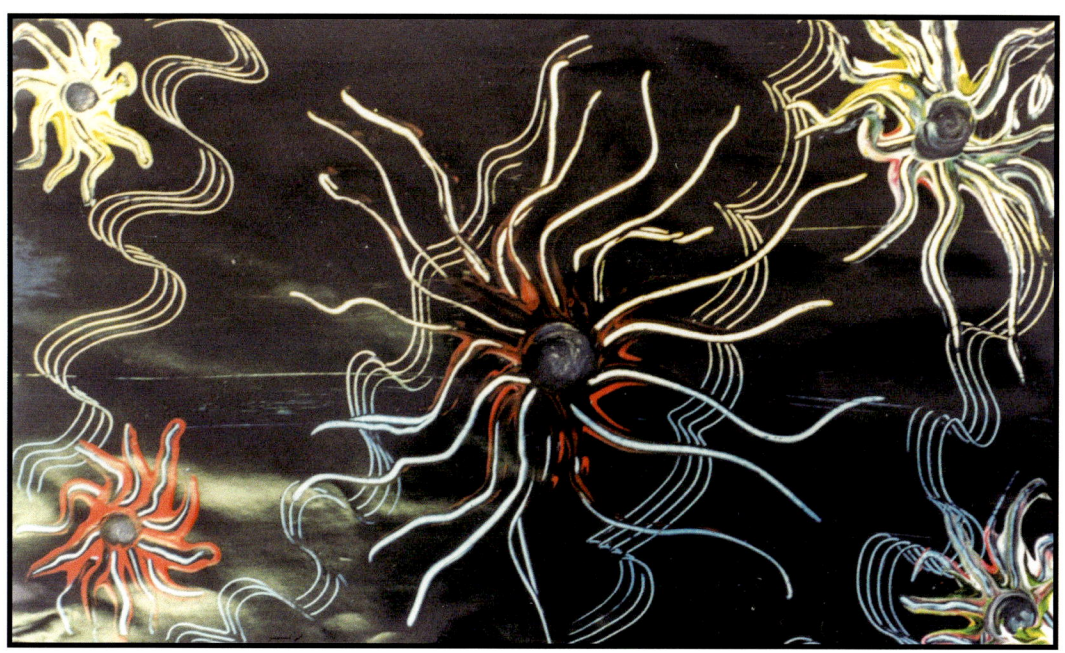

Bradley J 10

Shanna B 9

THE PARENTS

Karen

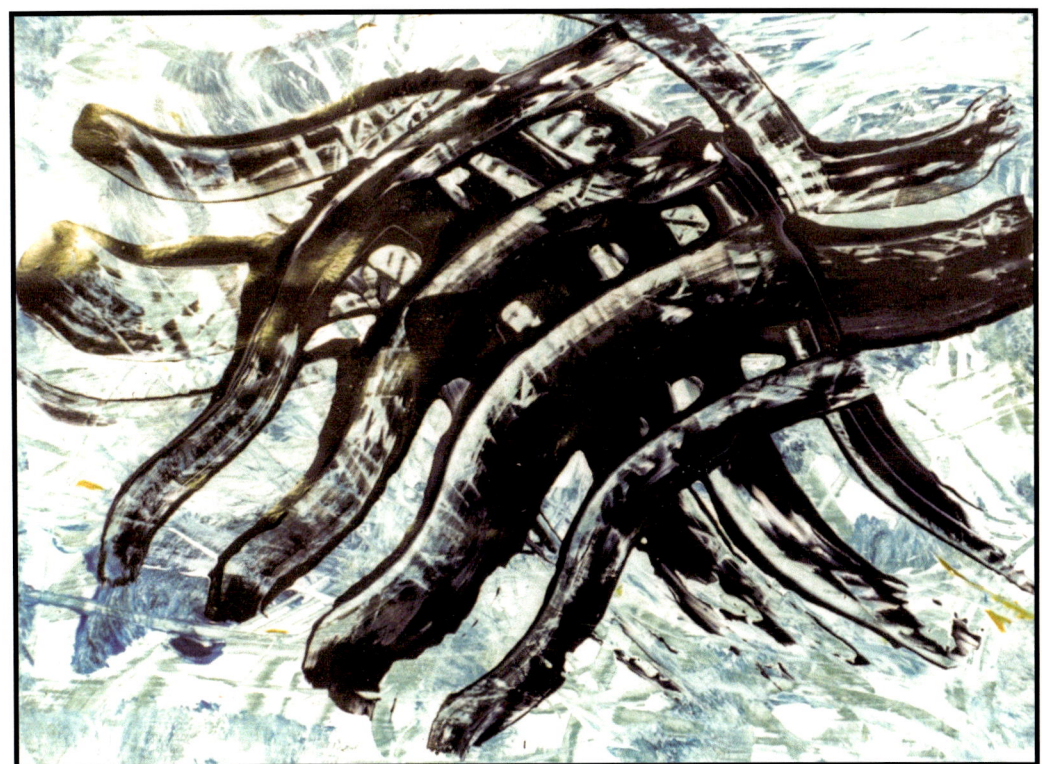

Karina

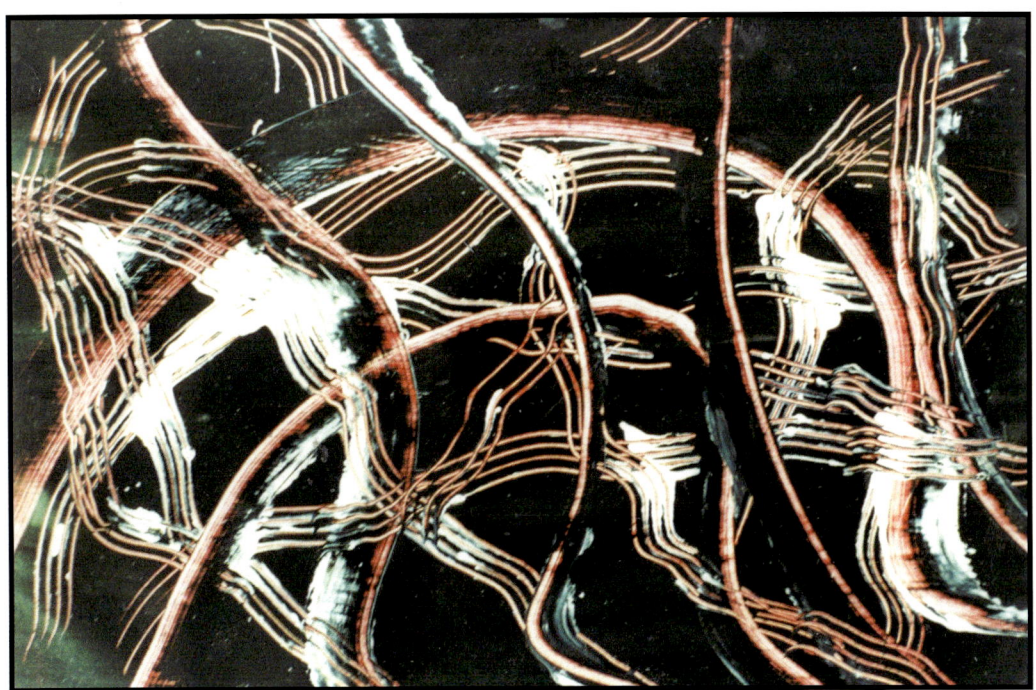

Linda

After our first workshop some of the fathers joined in alongside their children as they built up some simple Landscapes together. On every occasion a small group of child tutors freely gave a supporting hand to the parents, children, and teachers in attendance. A love of learning in a caring atmosphere was very much in evidence.

Annette

THE TEACHERS

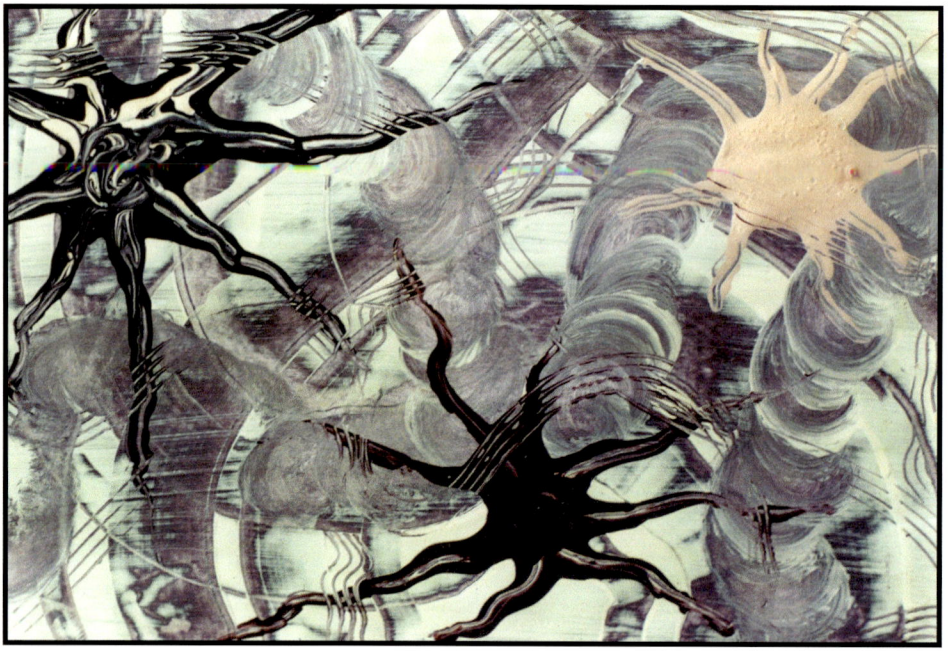

Mrs FYLE

Art in EDUCATION had found a new home. It was later suggested that other creative workshops of a literary and a mathematical nature could be considered for parents, children, and teachers. Big trees from small acorns grow.

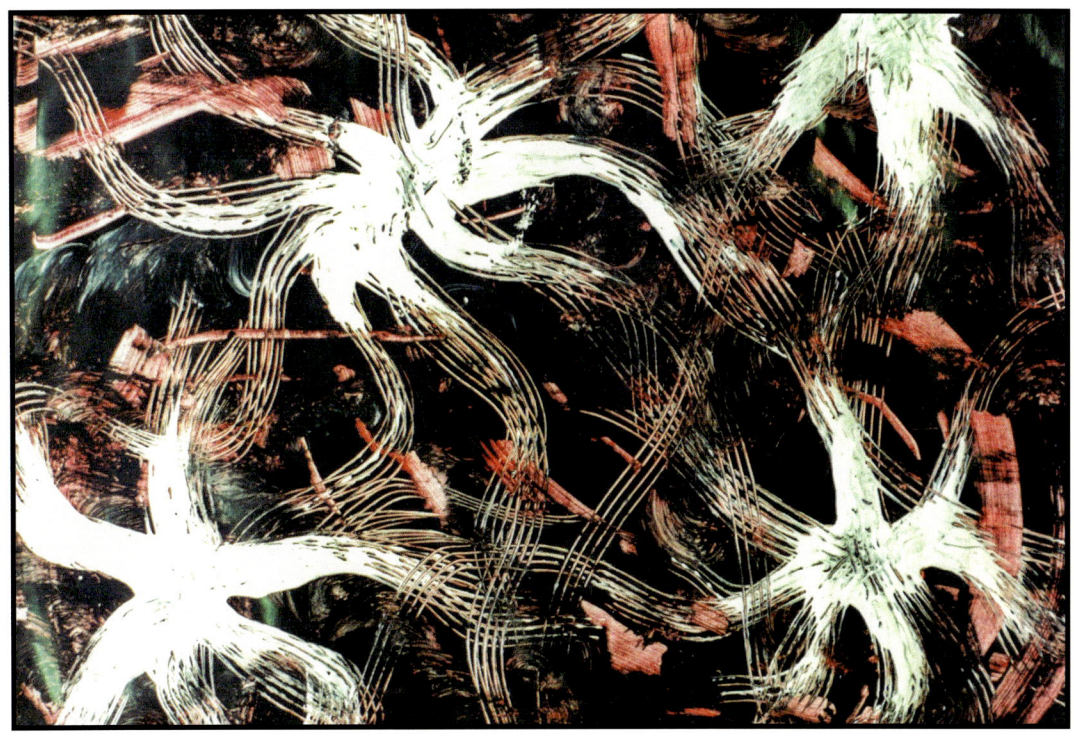

Mrs PALERMO

AN EXHIBITION OF PAINTINGS
ARISING OUT OF
OUT OF OUR RECENT WORKSHOP FOR CHILDREN
THEIR PARENTS AND TEACHERS
FUN WITH ABSTRACTS

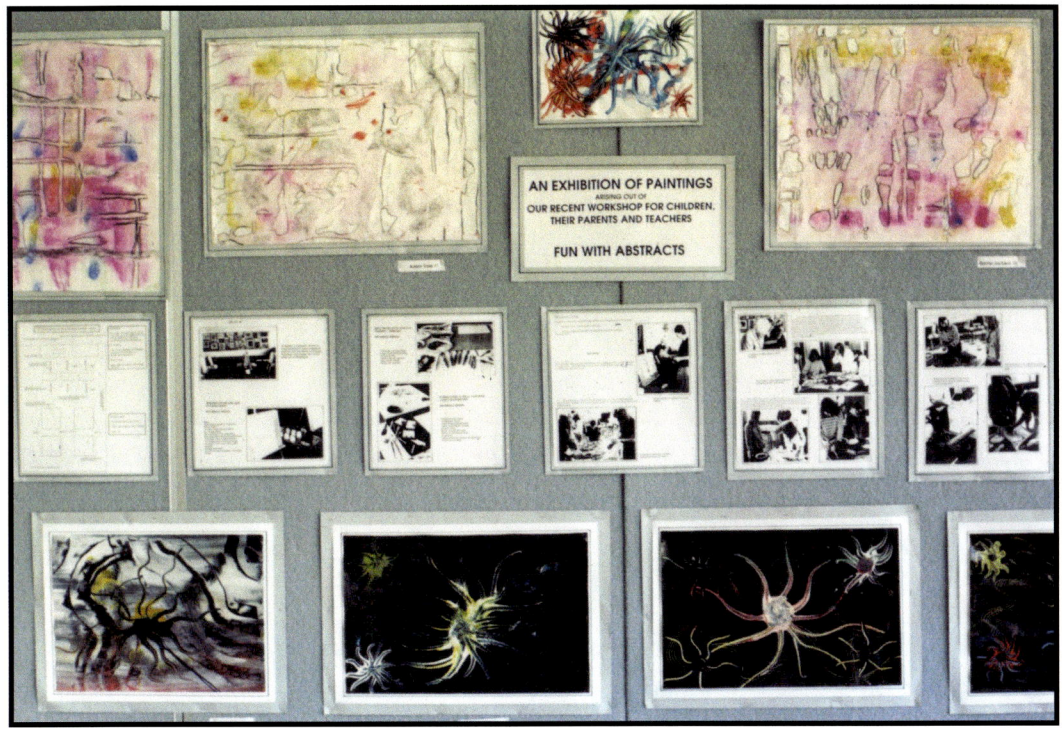

PORT ARTHUR

....

AN INSPIRATION FOR AN EXPLORATION
IN THE USE OF WATERCOLOURS

It was near the end of November 1997. The children in their final year of Primary School were to be treated to a day trip at the site of this convict penal settlement. The remaining year five children in our class did not like the idea at all.

"You said we will always be one class together and now you are going to split us up," one of them cried out.

"I am really sorry about this, and I did not want it to happen this way. I will offer you some very interesting activities on Monday to make up for your disappointment. Just think, it will be your turn next year," their teacher replied.

"Then we will be split up again," was the swift reply.

Their cries of protest haunted me as I boarded the bus for the two-hour trip to Port Arthur. Thirty-two year six children from two Grade five-six composite classes with four adults arrived at 10-30 am. The remaining year five children had to endure an uncertain day with a relief teacher.

The children took a short ferry trip around the bay to see an island graveyard and a prison for boys at Point Puer. Instead, I took a walk around the historic site made more notorious by the shocking shootings that had rocked our island state during the April of 1996. I paid my respects to the shelled remains of The Broad Arrows Café that was curiously un-noticed when the children had previously passed it by. After a silent moment by the memorial cross, I felt free to walk around the settlement.

The pervading gloomy shrouds of sadness were by then opaque enough to allow shafts of sunlight to shadow the skeletal remains of the convict ruins. My mind's eye was able to appreciate the perspective lines of the buildings in decay and the ironic beauty of their natural surroundings. My camera tried to capture the images of my heart and mind. Memories of a previous classroom experience with line and perspective, determined my desire to photograph the interesting lines of partially restored ruins. At the same time there remained a need to be at peace with my camera's capture of the aesthetic beauty of Port Arthur.

As soon as the children had completed their ferry trip, we were introduced to our Tour Guide, who for the next two hours escorted us around the historic settlement. There was no mention of the recent tragedy. Instead, the children were transported back to the first half of the 19th Century by a master storyteller.

The children were enthralled by the number of memorable stories as they drifted through many of the notable ruins and restored buildings. Some really enjoyed an exploration of the Commandant's house. Some were touched by the sudden appearance of the guide's wife who was dressed up as a servant and sang a sad lament for her long, lost convict lover.

However, most of the children just relished the hearing of gory stories of primitive medical practices in the hospital, the experience of fear and loneliness in a cell of solitary confinement or the sinister recollections in a ghostly basement morgue under the doctor's house.

BACK AT SCHOOL

We arrived back at school in the early evening of that Friday. On my desk the relief teacher had left a note.

It read, "The behaviour of the children was appalling. They were impossible to manage. They just did not want to be at school. I don't know how you could put up with this every day of the week." I filed his note in my diary for some later consideration.

We returned to school on the following Monday morning and my first job was to placate the year fives. I had promised them something special, so I chose "A CHRISTMAS CRACKER." This was a popular unit of work that was a success a couple of years back. The year fives had great fun with their artistic exploration, but they were also aware that I had planned for the year sixes an artistic response to our visit to Port Arthur. The year fives did not like the idea as they thought that we were a split class again. I had to find a way around the problem. We shall first deal with the Port Arthur response.

As soon as the colour photographs had been developed, copies of them were enlarged to an A4 size. The black and white enlargements accentuated line, perspective and shade and were an excellent guide for the children's drawings. The year sixes were invited to choose one or two of the black and white images and draw them with a soft 6B pencil on similar sized cartridge paper.

Some chose to draw their copies by free hand and some others preferred the use of grids. Most of the children chose to copy photos of convict ruins but no-one chose to draw The Broad Arrows Café, the major site of the massacre.

I had to be careful to spend equal time with both groups of children. The year fives were busy with their drawings of Santa having heaps of trouble delivering his presents as the sixers at the same time were pencil sketching some convict ruins. The teacher however, still felt uncomfortable with an apparently divided classroom. Over the next few days each of the two groups became more aware of the other's activities. Not long after, that we saw children from both groups having a try with both artistic explorations. We then witnessed children from both year groups sitting side by side showing the other the stages of their artistic journeys. The problem was solved. They had sorted it out themselves. We had become one class again and everyone was the happier for it.

There were only two weeks before our school year ended. There remained so much to do, so the teacher may have been a little overanxious in reaching a satisfactory conclusion to both artistic explorations. None the less, that did not excuse his rather poor response after looking at Danielle's drawing of the corner piece of the penitentiary. It was obvious that Danielle had taken great care with her drawing, and it was surprising that her teacher had not sighted her work earlier and provided a more appropriate and timely comment. Instead of acknowledging her fine efforts, her teacher was too quick to point out some errors of alignment with her three central windows.

"Dear me! What was she to do?" one might ask.

Her detailed drawing was near completion. She could hardly rub it out and start again.

A day or two later her teacher invited Danielle to use her drawing as a guide for a watercolour painting using fair dinkum watercolour paints from a tube. She declined to do so and that was a shame. No doubt she would have produced a lovely painting, but her teacher had shrivelled her enthusiasm enough to embark on any further painting. He had apologised to her, but it was too late. In retrospect, he should only have given praise for the appealing features of her drawing.

Had the teacher provided her with a more positive response, she might have accepted the challenge of play with real watercolours. If there remained a concern for the alignment of her windows, he could have quietly advised her so, had she progressed with a light sketch prior to her painting of the penitentiary.

Teachers should be more wary of untimely interventions and inappropriate comments. They should be more tolerant of errors and recognise them as part of the learning process. All learners should be less fearful of making mistakes. Errors should be seen as friendly signposts that remind us of where we are and point out some further directions for us to follow along our lifelong path of learning.

As the children completed their Port Arthur drawings, I suggested that some of them might like to try my watercolour paints for a painting using their pencil drawings as a guide.

Emma had nearly completed her drawing of the hospital

A GALLERY OF PORT ARTHUR DRAWINGS

Danielle C 11

Cade M 11

Adam V 12

Adrian D 12

Brent S 11

EXPLORING WATERCOLOURS

I brought along to school some of my watercolour paints, a pad of special paper suitable for watercolours and some of my expensive soft haired brushes.

While the children were busy one afternoon, I set up my watercolours and began a faint sketch using one of the photographs as a guide. It was not long before my work attracted the attention of a few children.

I was sampling their interest and at the same time introducing them to the next stage of this artistic exploration. About a dozen children were reminded to recognise the major lines in the photographs e.g.: the Skyline, the Buildings, and the major lines in the middle and foreground.

They were then shown how to faintly draw the major lines on to the special watercolour paper using an HB or 2B pencil. The word "FAINT" was stressed to ensure that the pencil lines would not have been seen through the watercolour paint.

Soon they were back to show me their preliminary sketches and they couldn't wait to squeeze the paint out of the tubes.

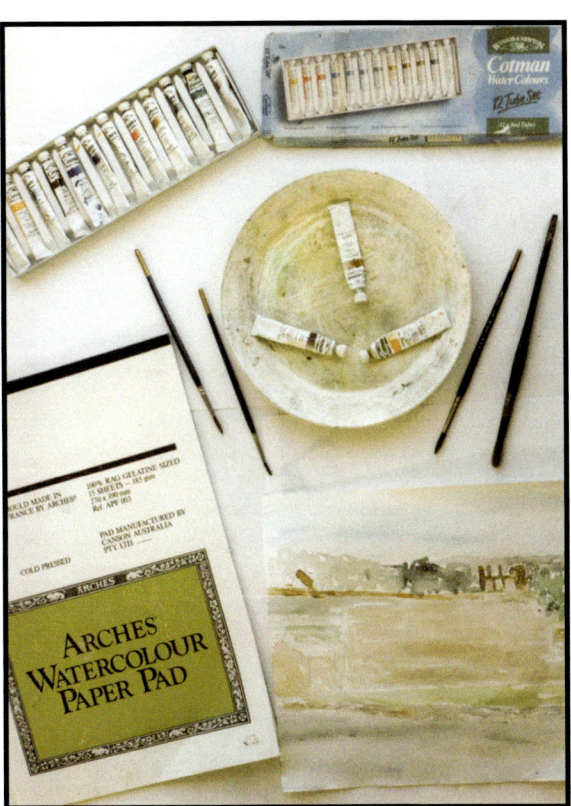

A basic set of suitable materials for painting water colours.

"Hold your horses!" cried MrE.

It was time for caution. None of the children had ever experienced these paints, quality soft haired brushes or watercolour paper before. Their teacher had never before used his watercolour materials at school. Therefore, it was wise to allow them a little exploration before they tried watercolour washes over our Port Arthur sketches.

Each child was provided with a small sheet of good quality watercolour paper. MrE then demonstrated that only a very small amount of paint, perhaps equivalent to half the amount of toothpaste one would put onto a toothbrush, was to be squeezed from the tube into the mixing tray. It was amazing that so little paint could spread so far.

Sharyn enjoyed the mixing of watercolour paints with water.

Their teacher showed them the delicate handling of a large soft haired brush as it was carefully dipped in water and gently brushed across a patch on the paper. While the paper was still wet a smaller brush was dipped into the water and then its tip gathered only a speck of watercolour paint before it was lightly brushed over the wet patch in left to right movements. The paint runs were amazing. They just could not wait to try it themselves.

So, off the adventurers explored.... They were reminded from time to time to be gentle with MrE's brushes and be sparing with the paint. All six of them brushed wet paint over wet paper to create runs.

"It's a bit like when we were running water through powder paint," suggested Malinda.

Some of them tried superimposing wet paint over wet paint and wet paint over dried paint. There seemed so many avenues for exploration. Their continued discoveries were to them far more exciting and meaningful than making simple copies of the well - intentioned examples set by their teacher.

Malinda tried a dash of salt.

"Try a sprinkle of salt over the wet paint," suggested their teacher for a little extra fun.

The explorers continued with their discoveries, and it was not long before they had covered their paper with fascinating patches of watercolour.

"Can we have some more paper MrE?"

"Well, if you do, we will not have enough paper for our Port Arthur watercolours. Besides another group of six should have their turn now," replied their teacher.

A couple of days later a dozen children were ready for their first sky washes with watercolour.

Cade superimposed a further colour over his first colour wash

TWO SAMPLES OF PRIMARY EXPLORATIONS WITH WATER COLOURS

A

The effect of salt can be clearly seen at the bottom right of sample A and at the bottom left of sample B.

"Oh! Look what the salt has done to my little wash," exclaimed Malinda "It's gone all speckled like..." she added before Cade joined in and said,

"That looks fantastic. It would have taken ages to try and do that with a brush. I wonder how we can do that in a real painting."

"I was thinking the same thing Cade," added MrE. "I have never seen anything like it before."

"You know what! I'm going to get my own watercolours and my first painting will be a watercolour abstract using salt," concluded Cade.

B

THE WATERCOLOURS OF PORT ARTHUR

Each child had easy access to the colour photograph of their choice safely protected within a plastic sleeve. Also available were half a dozen soft haired brushes of varying size. Nearby lay a paint mixing tray with small amounts of paint, cartridge paper for testing of mixed colours, a container of clean water and of course some A4 sheets of watercolour paper. The restricted number of brushes only allowed three children to work at a time. It was also easier for the teacher to keep an eye on their progress whilst he was working with the rest of the class.

We began with a sky wash. The sky space was lightly brushed with water before it was brushed over with previously mixed shades of sky colours. Some children revisited the idea of creating patches of sky blues and greys and left intermittent spaces for suggested cloud. Some kept it simple by brushing a shade or two of blue across the paper. Brush strokes were light and generally moved in left to right motions across the paper and back again. Gradually the brush strokes would have descended from the top of the paper down towards the skyline.

After a light pencil sketch of the major outlines Cade proceeded with a sky and foreground wash.

Mitchell had reached the stage for superimposing details over his painting of the Guard Tower.

As one approached the skyline, spaces between the brush stokes would have narrowed. The paint was thinned so that it helped us to reach and feel into the picture's distance. The children then would have tried a foreground wash towards the bottom of their sheet that suggested a grassy pasture. Over the wet surface they might have applied gentle brush strokes with mixture of greens, browns, and yellows. The mixing of colours was strongly recommended. If we used the green straight out of a tube, the effect would have been far too strident and would have taken from us a natural and soft pastel feel of the painting. We had to be always sparing with our use of paint on the brush and let the water do the work for us. It was far better to have understated an application of well diluted paint. If the painting appeared to be too pale and likely to fade, we could have superimposed some gentle brush stokes at a later stage. This kind of painting was a delicate matter and not for the heavy handed. It was far different from our use of Acrylics and The Risdon Vale Arts Group use of oil paints.

There should have been no need for panic if an error of judgement allowed too rich a colour tone. A clean brush dipped in water could have been gently brushed across the offending area and thus softening the blow.

The middle background was then painted after the sky wash and the washed foreground had dried. It could have been covered with a light wash of yellowy browns or a mix of those soft colours which could have been directly applied with a wet brush on to the dry paper.

Both Adrian and Luke superimposed detail over a dried background.

It was then time to paint the main subject... e.g., The Convict buildings. The children looked closely at the protected colour photographs. They easily recognised the variety of colour tones within the brick and sandstones that bathed in early summer sunlight or those which remained within the shade of an abundance of English trees. Tones of tans and light browns were mixed and tested before the suitable colours for buildings were brushed over the appropriate places with a well-watered soft haired brush. Even before the paint had dried a further tone could have been superimposed over the previous colour tone thus giving us a mottled look of brick and sandstone. Our paintings would have been completed by the addition of detail to the buildings with a fine lined soft haired brush.

It naturally followed that some children wished to try a second painting of Port Arthur. Some wished to paint a picturesque landscape while others wished to tackle another convict building. This, they were permitted to do as long it did not prevent anyone else having their first try with watercolours.

The teacher mostly would have acted as an unobtrusive advisor whenever it was possible. The children would have sought reassurance for what they were trying to do. They may have asked for supportive direction in overcoming a difficult moment. By this time of the year, they were well skilled in their mutual seeking and giving of support.

Brent added the finishing touches to his painting of the Penitentiary.

Sometimes they were able to watch their teacher at work on his own painting of Port Arthur and then they try to emulate some of his developing skills. Enthusiastic observers were often reminded of the need for the gentle touch of the brush and of the gentle art of mixing watercolour paint. Our recently acquired skills were in stark contrast with the bravado shown early in the school year with our handling of bristle brushes and acrylic paints. By the end of the year the mutual respect and understanding we had of each other together as learners and teachers, illuminated and strengthened the quality of our learning environment far beyond of the world of our artistic explorations.

Through all of this, the teacher had to resist the temptation to brush his own skills over the children's paintings. This would have dangerously eroded the degree of ownership the child had for his or her painting. It was far better for the teacher to have demonstrated the point on a piece of testing paper. Just look at the photographs of the children painting. Their testing sheets are clearly seen close by. They were, for us all, the painter's friend. No doubt that some of the patches of paint on their testing sheets might have been brushed by their teacher or by another supportive being.

We were not too self-conscious about our work. We were not too fearful of making mistakes as we had no high expectations. These were our first classroom experiences with watercolours. Even though we were just testing the waters, we were proud of our achievements. We were aware of errors of line, colour choice and brush strokes but we had built a solid foundation for future experience whether that be in next year's classroom, at a High School or as a newly found leisure activity. I already knew that some of the children had placed their orders for paints, brushes, and paper with Santa.

Emma painted her middle ground detail by using a wet brush over dry untouched paper.

A GALLERY OF WATERCLOURS OF PORT ARTHUR

Brent S 11

Adrian D 12

Cade M 11

Emma J 11

Luke C 12

Mitchell B 11

A CHRISTMAS CRACKER

On the following school day, I met the year fives in the Reading Corner for a chat.

"How was Friday?" I asked.

"It was awful MrE. He made us do worksheets all day and we had to sit in our places all day long. It was so boring. We started to play up after a bit," said one of them.

"It was not just us, there were the other grade fives too. They were just as bad," added another.

"It must have been pretty bad as he left me a note about your appalling behaviour. He said it was the worst he had ever seen. Now he will go to other schools and tell them how bad you were. It will give us a bad name."

"Oh, I'm sorry MrE. We are all sorry. We did not think of that."

"I will let it be for now. I have brought us together to also talk about that special activity I promised you last Friday."

Our school year was ending, and thoughts of Christmas came to mind. We all felt too tired for an extravagant swan song, so MrE felt more inclined to delve into his Christmas stocking and pull out a humorous idea or two. He asked the year fives to imagine the front end of a vehicle... It could have been a car, a train, an aeroplane... any mode of transport. The children were asked to draw it and then humanise some of its features.

E.g.: an imaginative view of a front end of a car could have revealed.......

Headlights ... as eyes, A radiator... as a nose, A bumper bar... as a mouth and so on.

The children really responded to the challenge. The teacher for a moment, thought that they were trying to make up for Black Friday. They really enjoyed several attempts at humanising an ever-increasing number of vehicles. They were encouraged to emphasise the interesting details by exaggeration. The year sixes had pricked up their ears and were aware of what might be in the offering. Those not immediately involved with the Port Arthur drawings quickly joined in with the Christmas activity. The class was a buzz again. Everybody was happy and their behaviour was just impeccable. They were motivated, they were once again active in giving and receiving support to each other. There was only ten days to go.

On the following day the children were asked to invite Santa Clause into their pictures. A caricature of Santa could have been on top, under, inside or even hanging from the vehicle. Their imaginative senses of humour took over and poor old Santa was caught in several amazing situations. The children were then asked to invent a suitable caption that would capture Santa's thoughts on meeting such situations. Much laughter permeated our classroom as the children naturally shared their emerging pictures with each other. They all thought it to be a cracker of a Christmas idea. The use of pastels and charcoal proved to be a popular medium as that speeded up production.

A GALLERY OF SANTAS

"HELP! Where's the brakes on this thing,".

Danielle C 11

"Help I can't stop this train".

Adrian D 12

"Help I'm stuck on this damn chain,".

Cade M 11

"This is ten times better than the sleigh,".

Brent S 11

'Slow down ......my reindeer don't go this fast!'

Julian S 11

"Oh no I should have used the reindeers,".

Brent S 11

'Oh no I've left my sack in the blimp'.

Mitchel B 11

"Please Sir, we want some more...."

"Some more! Well, let me see," said MrE, having to think on his feet.
"Well.... Imagine that Santa had found the roof of the house too slippery for his feet or perhaps he was stuck trying to find his way down the chimney. I wonder what might have happened once he was inside the house?"
The suggested ideas had sparkled them up again. It was not long before they created their own impossible situations for the luckless Santa. Their ideas seemed to flow from one to another and their pictures and captions tapped into their infectious, irresistible, and childlike humour.

"Oh no! Mrs. Claus said I was getting too fat,".

Danielle C 11

"I need to go to Jenny Craig,".

Sharyn G 10

'I Need To
Go On A Diet And Fast'

Jessica W 10

"I'm not going to have a very nice landing,".

Cade M 11

"Oh no!
not the Holly bush again!".

Adrian D 12

"Don't just stand there Rudolph help me!".

Joshua P 11

"I shouldn't have another ...HIC ...HIC ...glass of wine."

Julian S 11

"Oh, dear I've had too much to eat and drink,".

Luke C 12

"Oh no there's soot all over the floor again."

Malinda B 11

I was becoming aware that the year sixes were dominating the show, so I called the year fives over for another meeting in the Reading Corner.

"I wonder what I can do to make this Christmas activity special for you. I realise that it was to be your treat in the first place. Now what shall we do?

The shrugging of shoulders was their only reply.

"Look I have an idea. It is just for you to do. I have some A4 cardboard sheets here and I'll show you how to bend them in half using a ruler and the back end of a pair of scissors."

After my demonstration I suggested that they take a walk down to the Teacher Aides room and ask them to reduce the size of their Santa pictures by half. A few minutes later they had returned, and their faces looked a little brighter.

"After your sheets of cardboard have been folded in half, they could be made into Christmas cards by sticking your reduced Santa pictures on the front of the folded card.

"That's a lovely idea MrE. Can we do it now?"

"Of course, you can, but be quick about it. You have only a couple of days before the holidays. "You might like to trim a centimetre border off the edges of your picture before you stick it on the card. That will give you a nice border around your picture of Santa. Inside the folded card you might like to write a Christmas message."

Off they went to 'Happy land' to complete their cards. I only managed to sight a few of the completed ones. Most of them found their way home that very day.

The penultimate day had arrived. It was time for a cleanup. All our art utensils were cleaned and put away for the next year. Our displays around the school were taken down and the owners placed their works into their Art Folders that were soon to be taken home. The walls looked so bare. Voices seemed to echo from wall to wall. Suddenly there was a saddened feeling of loss as something special had come to an end.

Throughout the last day there were flurries of intense activity followed by moments with nothing to do except the playing of games both inside and outside. The furniture was stacked to one side of the room and then there was a final assembly where the year sixes were given their fitting farewell. Back in our sterile classroom we waited for the final bell to ring out the end of another school year.

MrE began to speak, "I just want to say well done and thank you for making this year so special for me. You have......"

The siren sounded. A cacophony of noise erupted as the excitable shrieks of children ricocheted from wall to wall across the empty room. Backs were slapped and shirts were autographed with marker pens. The noise then spread into the corridor. A few children lingered for a little while but soon there was an eerie silence. Mr E stood alone by his desk and gazed upon some presents and cards that the children had generously given him. He picked up a large brown envelope opened it and there before him was a Christmas card from Danielle, the girl that he had unwisely criticised for the incorrect alignment of windows in her drawing of the penitentiary just two weeks before. It depicted Santa having a difficult time delivering his presents. On it she had written, "To MrE, Thank you for two wonderful years at Risdon Primary School."

He smiled as he gathered his gifts and photographic records. It was time to go. He was in need of the comforts of his own home.

ACKNOWLEDGEMENTS

First and foremost, I must thank the children who were in my care at Risdon Vale Primary School from 1996 until my retirement in 2000. Without their wonderful contributions, this book would have not been possible. Thanks also to their parents for their support and for giving permission for me to take photographs and use children's work samples for this book.

Thanks also to the school staff at that time for their support. Particularly, I must thank Brendon Kelly who as principal, provided me with much support and encouragement. He just loved to be part of our excursions and often joined the class as we pursued our numerous explorations. The teacher aides must also be thanked, for their tireless efforts in and out of the classroom.

I must now thank my son Jonathan, who rang me for assistance in providing some creative explorations for his ten-year-old daughter during the 2020 Tasmanian Covid lockdown. That proved to be the catalyst for me to revisit the writing of this book about the benefits of artistic explorations. He also played a leading role with the restoration of the photographs.

Several people read my earlier manuscript and offered support, encouragement, and advice. Thanks to Sue Hobeck and her daughter Jesse, both former schoolteachers, and Louise Whitehead, a former psychologist for their support and encouragement. Thanks to my brother-in-law Mike, an author of several books, and his wife Angela for their support, advice, and encouragement. Frequent discussions on Skype to England will always be remembered with gratitude. Thanks to Terry Aulic, Harry Quick, both former teachers and federal politicians for their interest and advice. Thanks also to Clive Tilsley, the director of Fuller's Bookshop for his early advice and encouragement. Thanks to Marcus Gardner of Print Division, Hobart, for his cover design.

Special thanks to Hugo McCann, a former Dean of Education at the University of Tasmania and his wife Ida, a former drama in education teacher, for their continued support and advice over several years. Hugo was kind enough to write the forward for this book.

Lastly, I must give special thanks for the love and support of my wife Janet. She has read most of the manuscripts, put up with my absences as I worked on "A FLOWING THROUGH", and has been such a wonderful rock for me to fall back upon.

David Esling May 2022